LIVING THROUGH

WORLD WAR I

Nicola Barber

Chicago, Illinois

www.capstonepub.com
Visit our website to find out more information about Heinemann-Raintree books.

To order:
☎ Phone 888-454-2279
🖥 Visit www.capstonepub.com
  to browse our catalog and order online.

Edited by Andrew Farrow, Laura Knowles, and Megan Cotugno
Designed by Steve Mead
Original illustrations © Capstone Global Library Ltd
Picture research by Ruth Blair
Production by Eirian Griffiths
Originated by Capstone Global Library Ltd
Printed and bound in the USA

15 14 13 12 11
10 9 8 7 6 5 4 3 2 1

Library of Congress Cataloging-in-Publication Data

Barber, Nicola.
  World War I / Nicola Barber.
    p. cm.—(Living through—)
  Includes bibliographical references and index.
  ISBN 978-1-4329-6001-8 (hb)—ISBN 978-1-4329-6010-0 (pb) 1. World War, 1914-1918—Juvenile literature. I. Title. II. Title: World War One.
  D522.7.B27 2012
  940.3—dc22   2011015931

Acknowledgments

We would like to thank the following for permission to reproduce photographs: akg-images pp. 5, 43 (ullstein bild), 56; © Corbis p. 32; Corbis pp. 10 (© Bettmann), 15 (© Hulton-Deutsch Collection), 26 (© Bettmann), 28 (© Bettmann), 35 (© Hulton-Deutsch Collection), 49 (© Hulton-Deutsch Collection), 51 (© Bettmann), 53 (© Bettmann), 54 (© K.J. Historical), 59 (© Bettmann); Getty images pp. 17 (Hulton Archive), 25 (Hulton Archive), 30 (Buyenlarge), 41 (George C. Beresford/Stringer), 45 (Time Life Pictures/Mansell); Mary Evans pp. 9, 37, 46; National Library of Australia p. 21; Photolibrary pp. 61 (The Print Collector), 62 (The Print Collector).

Cover photograph of a British solider eating his dinner in the trenches during World War I reproduced with the permission of Corbis/© Underwood & Underwood.

We would like to thank A P Watt Ltd for their permission on behalf of The Literary Executors of the Estate of H G Wells to reproduce an extract from H G Wells, *The War That Will End War* (Frank & Cecil Palmer, 1914) on p. 17.

We would like to thank John Allen Williams for his invaluable help in the preparation of this book.

Every effort has been made to contact copyright holders of any material reproduced in this book. Any omissions will be rectified in subsequent printings if notice is given to the publisher.

Disclaimer

All the Internet addresses (URLs) given in this book were valid at the time of going to press. However, due to the dynamic nature of the Internet, some addresses may have changed, or sites may have changed or ceased to exist since publication. While the author and publisher regret any inconvenience this may cause readers, no responsibility for any such changes can be accepted by either the author or the publisher.

CONTENTS

Words printed in **bold** are explained in the glossary.

THE WAR'S ORIGINS

In 1871 Otto von Bismarck, then prime minister of Prussia, achieved his life-long ambition. The Franco-Prussian War (1870–71) was the last in a series of wars and campaigns that resulted in Bismarck's dream of creating a unified Germany. Under the **treaty** that ended the war, France lost the territories of Alsace and Lorraine to Germany, and this caused deep and continuing resentment among the French.[1] The German Empire was established with Bismarck as its chancellor and Wilhelm I of Prussia as its kaiser (emperor). The rise of a united Germany sparked new rivalries that laid the seeds for World War I— a war whose outcome still influences world events today.

ALLIANCES AND TREATIES

The other European powers at the time—Austria-Hungary, Great Britain, France, and Russia—regarded this new empire with some unease. Bismarck, meanwhile, embarked on a new policy to protect Germany and to maintain peace in Europe. One of his concerns was the region known as the **Balkans** (see the map on page 7). Not only was the rule of the **Ottoman Empire** being challenged by **nationalist** movements there, but both Austria-Hungary and Russia were trying to gain power in the region. Another worry was France. Bismarck knew that one day the French would seek revenge for their humiliating defeat in 1871.

Bismarck's solution was to make **alliances** to try to isolate France. He signed agreements with Austria-Hungary in 1879, and with both Austria-Hungary and Italy in 1882 (the "Triple Alliance"). Bismarck knew that any alliance between France and Russia would be particularly dangerous for Germany. If there were a war, Germany would be forced to fight on two fronts at once. Therefore, in 1887, he negotiated a secret treaty with Russia, called the Reinsurance Treaty.[2]

WILHELM'S *WELTPOLITIK*

In 1888 Wilhelm II succeeded his grandfather as kaiser of the German Empire. Wilhelm II had little time for Bismarck's cautious strategy of diplomacy and secrecy, and he forced the chancellor to resign in 1890. Wilhelm had already decided not to renew the Reinsurance Treaty with Russia. This opened the way for Russia to form a new alliance with France, which it promptly did in 1894. Wilhelm's vision was for Germany to become a major global power through a policy known as *Weltpolitik* ("world policy"). In pursuit of this policy, Wilhelm wanted to acquire territories overseas as German **colonies**. He also decided to build a German navy that would rival that of Britain in size and strength (see pages 8–9). In these aims, Kaiser Wilhelm was backed up by his new chancellor, Bernhard von Bülow, and his naval adviser, Alfred von Tirpitz.

BIOGRAPHY

Otto von Bismarck,
1815–1898

BORN: Prussia

ROLE: Prime minister of Prussia and imperial chancellor (1871–90). He was responsible for uniting most German-speaking kingdoms and states in Europe into one empire. As imperial chancellor, his aim was to maintain peace in Europe, to allow the new German Empire to flourish.

DID YOU KNOW?
Bismarck introduced the first health insurance program in Europe, including insurance for workers against accidents, sickness, and old age. He had a political motive, though. His motive was fear of the rise of **socialism** in Germany. These programs were designed to stop people from joining the increasingly popular socialist parties.

IMPERIALISM

The end of the 19th and beginning of the 20th centuries saw an upsurge in **imperialism**, as European powers scrambled to gain control of overseas colonies, mainly in Africa and Asia. Imperialism is the dominance of a powerful state over another, usually weaker, state, often by use of military force.

Some countries were already established imperial powers. By the 19th century, Britain, for example, had an empire that included colonies in Australia, India, and North America. Its empire gave Britain a huge commercial advantage. Not only were its colonies sources of cheap raw materials, but they also provided ready markets for goods manufactured in Britain. To maintain this commercial advantage, Britain had a powerful navy to patrol the world's seas and oceans. Throughout the 19th century, Britain remained in "splendid isolation," unwilling to become involved in alliances with other European powers.

The turn of the 19th century saw Britain's supremacy and isolation being challenged. Other countries wanted overseas colonies. Germany, Italy, Belgium, the United States, and Japan all joined in the rush to lay claim to parts of Africa and Asia.[3] Germany was not alone in building a naval fleet to rival that of Britain. France, Japan, and the United States also built up large navies of their own. In 1902 Britain signed its first international alliance with Japan, followed in 1904 by a treaty with France (the "*Entente Cordiale*") and, in 1907, one with Russia.[4]

SUSPICION AND CRISES

Britain's international alliances were made primarily to safeguard its colonies. Among other issues, the Anglo-Japanese treaty addressed British fears about its commercial interests in East Asia. The *Entente Cordiale* cleared up disputes over territories in Africa—Britain kept its claim over Egypt, while France kept its control over Morocco. But in Germany, Kaiser Wilhelm viewed these new alliances with suspicion. The Anglo-Russian agreement of 1907—which aimed to settle disputes over territorial claims in Persia (Iran), Tibet, and Afghanistan—only made Germany feel more encircled. Two rival **power blocs** were emerging in Europe: the Triple Entente (Britain, France, and Russia) and the Triple Alliance (Germany, Austria-Hungary, and Italy).

In 1908 trouble erupted in the Balkans, when Austria-Hungary took control of the provinces of Bosnia and Herzegovina. This act was greeted with outrage both in the neighboring country of Serbia and in Russia, which backed Serbia. In 1911 a crisis in Morocco further highlighted the tensions between the European powers. Germany sent a gunboat into the port of Agadir, in Morocco, to challenge French supremacy in the region. The confrontation was eventually resolved diplomatically.

European attention moved quickly back to the Balkans. War broke out in 1912, when an alliance made up of Bulgaria, Serbia, Greece, and Montenegro (known together as the Balkan League) finally brought about the end of Ottoman (Turk) rule in Europe. However, the treaty that ended the war pleased none of the members of the Balkan League. War broke out again in 1913, when Bulgaria attacked Serbia. This ended with Serbia making considerable territorial gains.

△ The Balkan Wars resulted in the Ottoman Empire losing most of its European territories.

THE NAVAL ARMS RACE

Kaiser Wilhelm II wanted the prestige and commercial advantages of an overseas empire. In order to acquire and maintain far-flung colonies, he needed a powerful navy. But both Wilhelm and his naval adviser, Alfred von Tirpitz, knew that Germany could not build a navy to equal the power and size of the British fleet.

Instead, Tirpitz proposed the "risk theory." In this theory, Germany would build a navy large enough to pose a risk to the British in battle, and therefore to deter Britain from going to war with Germany.[5] Tirpitz thought that the presence of a large German fleet would be enough to increase Germany's maritime influence and allow the kaiser to "conduct a great overseas policy."[6]

GERMAN CONSTRUCTION

The First German Naval Bill was passed in 1897. It provided for the construction of 19 battleships, 12 large cruisers, 30 small cruisers, and assorted smaller ships. A second bill, passed in 1900, doubled the number of battleships to be built.[7] Another development was the construction of the Kiel Canal, a waterway to link the Baltic Sea and the North Sea. Wilhelm II officially opened it in 1895. Between 1907 and 1914, the canal was widened to allow the biggest of the new German battleships to pass along it.[8] The canal proved an important link for the German Baltic and North Sea fleets.

BRITAIN'S RESPONSE

Britain's response to all of this German activity was to reinforce and reorganize its own navy. It was now safe to return several ships from the Pacific to boost naval defenses in waters nearer home, thanks to the Anglo-Japanese treaty of 1902. These reforms were carried out under the leadership of Admiral John Fisher.[9] Fisher was also responsible for the construction of the world's first "all-big-gun" battleship, the HMS *Dreadnought*.

The construction of the *Dreadnought* was completed in December 1906. This battleship was faster and armed with bigger guns than any previous battleships. It immediately made all the existing ships in the British and German navies out-of-date and obsolete. Kaiser Wilhelm recognized that HMS *Dreadnought* was the "armament of the future."[10] The race was now on to produce more of this powerful new type of ship. The *Dreadnought* gave its name to this new class of battleship.

Germany secretly launched its own **dreadnought** program in June 1906.[11] In 1908 Britain discovered that Germany was in the process of building four dreadnoughts, while only two were under construction for the British navy. The British government and navy chiefs disagreed about committing large amounts of money to dreadnought construction. The navy wanted to build six dreadnoughts, while the government wanted only four— with four more later, if needed. The British press stirred up patriotic fervor with slogans such as "We want eight and we won't wait."[12] All eight dreadnoughts were eventually built.

HMS *Dreadnought*

In service: 1906–1918   *Length*: 527 feet (160.6 m)

Beam (width): 82 feet (25 m)   *Crew*: 773

Speed: 21 knots   *Armament*: 10-x-12 in. (305-mm) guns

Active service: On March 29, 1915, HMS *Dreadnought* rammed and sank the German submarine U-29.

You can find out more about this ship by visiting www.history.navy. mil/photos/sh-fornv/uk/uksh-d/dredt9.htm.

▷ The HMS *Dreadnought* was enormous, but it was built in just over a year, from 1905 to 1906.

1914

In the summer of 1914, Archduke Franz Ferdinand, the nephew of the Austrian emperor Franz Josef I, decided to visit the Bosnian capital, Sarajevo. Bosnia had been under Austria-Hungarian rule since 1908 (see page 7). This caused great resentment among many Bosnians. The **annexation** of Bosnia had prompted a rapid growth in terrorist groups, particularly among Serb nationalists who were dedicated to the overthrow of Austrian rule.[1] For the Serb population in Bosnia, the date of Franz Ferdinand's visit, June 28, was an unfortunate choice.[2] In the Serbian calendar, June 28 is Vidovdan, a national festival that commemorates a famous battle fought between the Serbs and the Turks in the 14th century.[3] Austrian diplomats warned Franz Ferdinand that he would be in grave danger if he visited Sarajevo on such a significant day, but the warnings were ignored.[4]

△ This is Archduke Franz Ferdinand and his wife, Sophie, in Sarajevo on June 28, 1914, pictured about an hour before they were both assassinated.

On the morning of June 28, Franz Ferdinand and his wife, Sophie, paraded through the streets of Sarajevo in an open-topped car. At one point, the car took a wrong turn and was forced to stop. A young man named Gavrilo Princep saw his chance. Stepping out of the crowd, he shot and killed both the archduke and his wife. Princep had links with the nationalist movement "Young Bosnia" and with a secret organization based in Serbia known as the "Black Hand." The death of Franz Ferdinand and his wife caused fury in Austria-Hungary. Although the Serbian government had nothing to do with the plot, the terrorists' involvement with the Black Hand gave Austria-Hungary the excuse it had long been looking for to assert its authority over Serbia.

A CHAIN OF EVENTS

Austria-Hungary consulted with its ally, Germany. Kaiser Wilhelm II promised to "stand behind" Austria-Hungary in its actions against Serbia. Germany expected such a war to be a localized affair, but it was prepared to take the risk of a full-scale European war. On July 23, 1914, Austria-Hungary issued Serbia with an ultimatum. Acting on the belief that Serbia was involved in the Sarajevo plot, the ultimatum made 10 demands aimed at ending Serbian terrorist activity. Serbia agreed to nearly all the demands. But Austria-Hungary insisted that Serbia must accept the whole document. On July 28, 1914, Austria-Hungary declared war on Serbia.[5]

Russia did not have a treaty with Serbia, but it was bound to its Serbian neighbors by strong religious and historical ties,[6] and it was concerned about increased Austro-Hungarian influence in the Balkans. The Russian **tsar** and government knew they could not stand and watch Serbia being bullied by Austria-Hungary. Russia was already prepared for war. When Austro-Hungarian forces began to bombard Belgrade, Serbia's capital, Russia announced the **mobilization** of its army—although it still hoped for a negotiated settlement.

Table of military strength of European states in 1914[7]

Country	Population	Mobilized army
Austria-Hungary	49,800,000	2,000,000
Germany	65,000,000	4,500,000
Russia	167,000,000	4,500,000
France	39,600,000	3,780,000
Britain	46,400,000	713,514

Germany viewed Russian mobilization as an act of aggression. In any case, it was required militarily to mobilize its forces if Russia did. If Germany did not mobilize, it would have no time to stop a Russian invasion. Even though Russia still hoped for a peaceful settlement, Germany declared war on Russia on August 1. At that point, Germany's military plan, the Schlieffen Plan (see box below), came into operation. Although the perceived threat to Germany was coming from Russia in the east, the first step of this plan was a rapid attack on France, in the west, through Belgium. On August 2, therefore, Belgium received an ultimatum from Germany demanding that it allow safe passage across its territory for the German army. As a **neutral** country, Belgium refused. On August 3, Germany declared war on France. That same night, the German army invaded Belgium.

The Schlieffen Plan

Named after the man who developed it, Count Alfred von Schlieffen, the Schlieffen military plan was the German response to the alliance between France and Russia of 1894 (see page 5). Germany feared a war on two fronts—against France in the west and Russia in the east—and this alliance sharpened that fear. Schlieffen knew that in the event of war, the mobilization of the Russian army would take several weeks (see page 22). His plan was to make use of this time to crush the French army, before concentrating forces in the east. Instead of attacking France along the heavily fortified French–German border, Schlieffen planned to send the German army on a rapid march through Belgium (see the map on page 13), which was a neutral country, and then swing south into France to capture Paris.[8]

The German attack on Belgium forced Britain to commit itself for the first time. Up until that point, the British foreign secretary, Edward Grey, had been working to end the crisis through mediation and diplomacy. But Germany's violation of Belgium's neutrality changed the situation. British leaders had long felt they could not permit such a powerful country to control the territory just across the narrow strait from them. Although Britain had no formal agreement with any country to involve it in the war, it did have a treaty (dating back to 1839) that committed Britain to Belgium's defense if that country were invaded. Britain declared war on Germany on August 4. In a matter of a few weeks, Europe had descended into war. Serbia, the initial cause of the crisis, was almost forgotten.

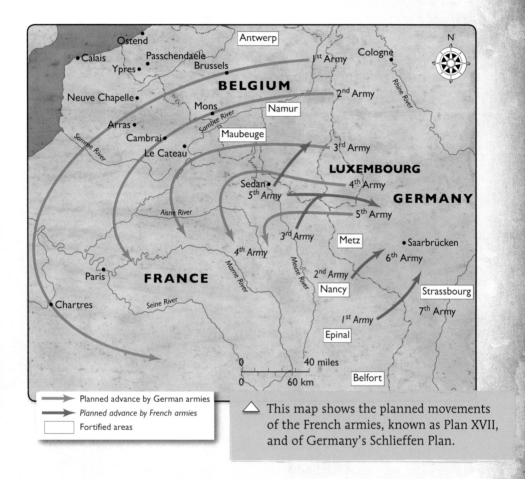

△ This map shows the planned movements of the French armies, known as Plan XVII, and of Germany's Schlieffen Plan.

THE BATTLE OF THE FRONTIERS

Speed of attack was central to the Schlieffen Plan. The plan was put into effect not by Schlieffen, who had retired in 1906, but by German **Chief of Staff** Helmuth von Moltke. During August 1914, German troops fought their way across Belgium, encountering serious resistance from the Belgian army, which slowed their progress long enough for the French and British to prepare their defenses. By August 20, the German troops had captured Brussels. Meanwhile, the French army was attacking along the French–German border and in southern Belgium. This series of clashes between the French and German armies became known as the Battle of the Frontiers (see the map above).

THE END OF THE SCHLIEFFEN PLAN

The British government sent an army, called the British Expeditionary Force (BEF), to France in early August. British troops first saw action alongside the French army at the Battle of Mons (August 23). This battle held up the German advance, but it ended with an **Allied** (French and British) retreat as the German army pushed onward. At this point, under Moltke's leadership, the Schlieffen Plan began to unravel. The speed of advance in the plan was a weakness. In many cases, supplies could not keep up with the movement of the troops. German soldiers, who had been almost continuously marching and fighting for several weeks, were becoming exhausted. Crucially, Moltke also decided to divert several divisions from the fighting in Belgium to help stop a Russian attack on the Eastern Front in East Prussia.

On August 28, Kaiser Wilhelm II ordered the German army to begin its advance on Paris.[9] The city emptied as its citizens fled and the French government moved to Bordeaux. The German army advanced into the valley of the Marne River, north of Paris. The Battle of the Marne (September 6–10) was the turning point for the Germans. Unable to withstand Allied attacks, the German army retreated about 40 miles (65 kilometers), finally digging a defensive line along the Aisne River. Broken by the failure of the Schlieffen Plan, Moltke was replaced by a new German chief of staff, Erich von Falkenhayn.

The British army

Before World War I, the British regular army was tiny compared to those of its European neighbors. Many regular soldiers were posted around the world, policing the colonies of the British Empire. In the years leading up to 1914, a small extra force of six infantry **divisions** was trained and equipped to form the British Expeditionary Force of just over 700,000. When war was declared, four of these divisions were sent to northern France to fight alongside the French army. At the same time, regular soldiers were recalled from their foreign posts. Minister for War Herbert Horatio Kitchener began his "call to arms" on August 11, 1914, to enlist volunteers for the army (see page 17). In late 1914 and early 1915, the army was also expanded by the arrival of troops from Britain's colonies, including Indians (see page 36–37), Canadians, Australians, and New Zealanders.[10]

THE FIRST BATTLE OF YPRES

During September 1914, attacks by the Allies on the German positions along the Aisne River proved fruitless. Attention turned instead to the area of land between the Aisne and the English Channel. Both sides tried to outmaneuver each other in a so-called "race to the sea," with the Germans trying to cut off the British Expeditionary Force from the Channel ports. The First Battle of Ypres, fought in October and November 1914, ended this phase of the fighting. Both the Germans and the Allies sustained heavy losses. By the end of the First Battle of Ypres, nearly all of the original members of the British Expeditionary Force had been killed.[11]

With winter setting in, the two sides fought themselves to a standstill. By the end of 1914, both the Allies and the Germans had dug themselves into lines of defensive trench systems, known as the Western Front, that stretched from the English Channel to the French border with Switzerland (see the map on page 38). The war of movement had ended, and one of **attrition** had begun.

▽ These Belgian troops are taking up their position along the bank of a canal during the First Battle of Ypres, 1914.

ENTHUSIASM FOR THE WAR?

The declarations of war were greeted with outpourings of patriotism around Europe. Crowds gathered in London, England, and other European cities. In Britain the foreign secretary, Edward Grey, gave a speech justifying British involvement in the war, which was greeted enthusiastically by members of **Parliament**. Britain's *Morning Post* newspaper of August 4 reported: "Members rose from their seats, cheered and cheered again, and wildly waved hats and handkerchiefs."[12] In an address to Parliament on August 6, 1914, Prime Minister Herbert Asquith stressed the moral basis for war, saying: "I do not believe any nation ever entered into a great controversy ... with a clearer conscience and a stronger conviction that it is fighting, not for aggression, not for the maintenance even of its own selfish interest, but ... in defense of principles the maintenance of which is vital to the civilization of the world."[13]

PROTEST AND PROPAGANDA

Yet enthusiasm for the war was not universal. Even some politicians who backed the war in public expressed their doubts in private. Foreign Secretary Grey famously remarked to a friend upon the outbreak of war that "The lamps are going out all over Europe; we shall not see them lit again in our lifetime."[14] Others were open in their opposition to war. These included members of the antiwar group the Union of Democratic Control,[15] and left-wing organizations such as the Independent Labour Party.[16] In a letter to the magazine *The Nation* on August 15, the British philosopher and **pacifist** Bertrand Russell wrote: "Against the vast majority of my countrymen ... in the name of humanity and civilization, I protest against our share in the destruction of Germany."[17]

The British government realized the need to ensure public support for its actions. The newspapers were largely supportive of the war effort. Nevertheless, the government quickly introduced the Defense of the Realm Act to impose press **censorship** (see page 54 for more about this). It also set up the War **Propaganda** Bureau to try to influence public opinion both at home and abroad. Recruits to this bureau included influential and well-known writers such as Thomas Hardy, H. G. Wells, Robert Bridges, Sir Arthur Conan Doyle, and J. M. Barrie.[18] As part of his work for the bureau, Wells published a book called *The War That Will End War*. As the title suggests, Wells justified this war by arguing that it would put an end to future wars, saying: "War is mortal conflict. We have now either to destroy or be destroyed. We have not sought this reckoning, we have done our utmost to avoid it; but now that it has been forced upon us it is imperative that it should be a thorough reckoning."[19]

The need for volunteers

Many people believed that the war would be "over by Christmas." Minister for War Kitchener thought differently. In August 1914, he launched a campaign, "Your Country Needs You," to recruit thousands of volunteers for the British army. "Who's Absent? Is It YOU?" and "Daddy, What did YOU do in the Great War?" were some of the poster slogans used to attract recruits.[20] The campaign was very successful. The first 100,000 men were enlisted within two weeks.[21] Before **conscription** was introduced in 1916, almost 2.5 million men had volunteered to serve in the British army.[22]

◁ Here, British men are on their way to join the army in 1914.

THE DARDANELLES AND GALLIPOLI

In October 1914, the Ottoman Empire (Turkey) had entered the war on the side of the **Central Powers** (Germany and Austria-Hungary).[1] In Britain, Winston Churchill, who was in charge of naval affairs, believed that the time was right to attack the Ottoman Empire. The Dardanelles Strait links the Aegean Sea with the Sea of Marmara, providing a route to the Black Sea and Russian ports. Churchill wanted to seize control of this important supply route. He also wanted to help the Russians by diverting Turkish troops away from battles in the east.[2] He hoped the prestige of a victory would persuade countries like Bulgaria to enter the war on the side of the Allies. From February 1915 until January 1916, the Allies fought to take control of the Dardanelles Strait and western Turkey (see the map at left).[3]

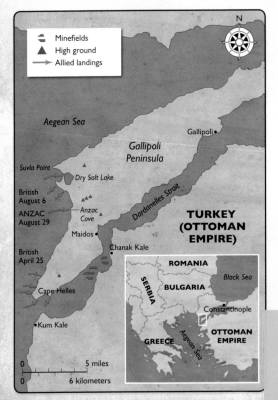

An Allied naval attack was launched in February 1915, but after losing three battleships, the navy retreated in March. In April, Allied ground troops began an attack on the Gallipoli Peninsula. They included some British, French, and Indian, but mostly **Anzac** (Australian and New Zealand) troops. Preparations for the landings at Cape Helles

◁ The Gallipoli Peninsula was the scene of fierce fighting in 1915.

and Ari Burnu (renamed Anzac Cove) were badly managed, and the Allied troops encountered fierce resistance from defending Turkish soldiers. There were many casualties, and the Allied troops were unable to move beyond the **beachheads** on which they had landed. New landings at Suvla Bay on the west coast in August led to more fierce fighting and heavy casualties, but no breakthrough.

RESIGNATION AND EVACUATION

In November 1915, Churchill resigned from the government. After a visit by Minister for War Kitchener to the peninsula, the decision was taken to evacuate all Allied troops. This took place over three weeks in December 1915 and January 1916, with remarkably few casualties. Overall, however, the campaign had been a costly failure. It had taken 480,000 soldiers away from the fighting on the Western Front, with 252,000 of these men being injured or killed. The Anzac troops suffered particularly badly— nearly 34,000 were injured or killed.[4] Although the campaign had diverted Turkish troops who would otherwise have been fighting elsewhere, it had failed to open up a supply route to Russia. It also helped to convince Bulgaria to join with the Central Powers rather than the Allies.[5]

BIOGRAPHY

Winston Churchill, 1874–1965

BORN: Blenheim Palace, Oxfordshire, England

ROLE: Churchill was a statesman and writer. In his early life he served in the army as a soldier and a journalist in India and Africa. He was elected to Parliament in 1900. During World War I he was first lord of the **Admiralty** (1911–15), returning to active service with the army in France after his resignation over Gallipoli. In 1917 he was appointed as minister of **munitions** and oversaw the development of the tank. During World War II (1939–45), he was again first lord of the Admiralty, and then prime minister (1940–45).

DID YOU KNOW? Churchill won the Nobel Prize for Literature in 1953, "for his mastery of historical and biographical description as well as for brilliant oratory [speeches] in defending exalted human values."

ALBERT JACKA

"He was a soldier with both physical and moral courage of the highest order.... He hated the necessity of war, but felt it to be a necessity; and he would see his job through." Rev. F. W. Rolland, January 1, 1937

One of the most famous of the Anzac troops who fought at Gallipoli was Albert Jacka. He joined the army in September 1914 and spent two months training in Egypt, before landing at Anzac Cove on April 26, 1915. Jacka and the rest of the Anzac troops then dug themselves into defensive trenches above the beach the best they could. On May 19, the Turkish defenders launched an attack that was designed to drive the invaders back toward the sea. However, Anzac observers had been watching Turkish preparations for the attack. When it started, the Anzac soldiers were ready for it. As wave after wave of Turks came toward the Anzac defenses, they were cut down by gunfire.

Anzac Day

In both Australia and New Zealand, the first day of the Gallipoli landings, April 25, is commemorated every year as "Anzac Day." On this day, Australians and New Zealanders now remember all their countrymen and women who have died serving their country.[6] Despite the military failure, the Gallipoli campaign left behind a powerful legacy. The courage and endurance of the Anzac troops gave a new sense of independence and pride, and it helped to foster a sense of national identity in both countries.[7]

In one part of the Anzac trench, however, the Turks did break through. This trench was guarded at one end by Lance Corporal Jacka. After firing warning shots for several minutes while reinforcements arrived, Jacka and three others attempted an attack on the Turks. The other Anzac soldiers were immediately hit and injured. Jacka quickly retreated to devise a new plan. Two bombs were thrown to create a diversion. In the noise and confusion, Jacka ran around a back way to the occupied trench, jumped in, and single-handedly killed several Turkish soldiers.[8]

HERO IN THE EAST AND THE WEST

For his bravery, Jacka was awarded the Victoria Cross—the highest military honor awarded by the British. He was the first Australian to receive this military honor in World War I. As such, he also received some money and a gold watch that had been promised by an Australian businessman to the first winner of the medal. He became an instant hero in Australia. His image was used on recruiting posters, and from that time his exploits were widely reported in the Australian newspapers.[9] After Gallipoli, he was sent to the Western Front. Once again, his bravery was outstanding. In one incident at Pozières, he led a small group of men to save 40 Australian soldiers who were being taken prisoner. During this exchange, Jacka was seriously wounded and was sent to a hospital in London. In September 1915, some newspapers reported that he had died, but the reports were untrue. For his actions in Pozières, he was awarded another high-level military honor, the Military Cross.

Jacka survived more action in France, and he eventually returned to Australia in 1919. He died in 1932. His funeral was attended by thousands of ex-Anzac troops.[10]

▷ In addition to being used for recruitment posters, Albert Jacka's heroic image was also used on posters urging the public to invest its money in the war effort.

He kept his Pledge

JACKA

YOU BUY PEACE BONDS

THE EASTERN FRONT

Just like Germany and France, Russia had a battle plan drawn up well before war broke out in 1914. "Plan 19" was devised by General Yuri Danilov in 1910, and it was based—correctly, as it turned out—on the belief that Germany would attack France before it attacked Russia. In response, Danilov planned a **pincer** movement on East Prussia, the easternmost province of the German Empire.[1] The plan was revised in 1912 because of fears of the threat from Austria-Hungary. In the event, two Russian armies were sent into action in East Prussia, while two remained in Russia to defend against any attack from Austria-Hungary.[2]

RUSSIAN DEFEATS

The 1st and 2nd Russian armies, commanded by General Paul von Rennenkampf and General Alexander Samsonov, marched into East Prussia in August 1914. Their forces outnumbered those of the opposing German forces by two to one.[3] The plan was for the two armies to meet and combine, pushing the Germans back. Rennenkampf's 1st army had initial victories at Stalluponen (August 17) and Gumbinnen (August 20). At this point,

The Russian Army

With a huge population (see page 11), Russia had large reserves of manpower to call upon for its army. But Russia's vast size meant that moving soldiers and equipment from one place to another was always a problem. The Germans had based the Schlieffen Plan on a calculation that the Russian army would take six weeks to mobilize.[4] In fact, the construction of new railroads in Russia had considerably cut down the time needed for mobilization.[5] In 1904–05, Russia's navy and Imperial Army had suffered a humiliating defeat in a war with Japan[6] (see pages 26–27). In the wake of this defeat, attempts were made to reorganize and reform the army. But many of the Russian generals found it difficult to modernize. For example, despite the development of powerful guns that could easily wipe out both horses and riders, the Russian Imperial Army continued to rely heavily on its **cavalry** in battle.[7]

This map shows the Eastern Front from 1914 to 1918. The battles on this front were fought across a huge area of Europe.

Rennenkampf stopped his army's advance in order to regroup. The Germans, meanwhile, were surrounding Samsonov's 2nd army. Unaware of the danger, Samsonov's situation was made worse when the Germans intercepted uncoded messages that made it clear that his army would not receive support from Rennenkampf's forces.[8] In the Battle of Tannenberg, the 2nd army was crushed by the Germans. Out of an army of 150,000 men, only about 10,000 escaped.[9] The rest were killed or taken prisoner. Samsonov shot himself, unable to face the consequences of the disaster.

The German commander, Paul von Hindenburg, now turned his attention to the Russian 1st army. At the First Battle of the Masurian Lakes, Rennenkampf was forced to retreat. By September 13, he had withdrawn all his troops from East Prussia. He did, however, mount a **counterattack** that forced the German army back once again, and he helped reclaim much of the ground Russia had lost in the previous battle.[10]

ATTACKS IN GALICIA

While Russia's 1st and 2nd armies were busy in East Prussia, its 3rd and 8th armies moved into Galicia, the northernmost province of Austria-Hungary (see the map on page 23). The Russians made rapid progress through Galicia in the fall of 1914. Austria-Hungary had, meanwhile, invaded Russian Poland.[11] By late in the year, the army of Austria-Hungary, now backed up by German forces, had established a defensive line along the Carpathian Mountains.

Poison gas

On January 31, 1915, a German attack on the Russian army was launched at Bolimov in Poland. This attack was designed to draw Russian attention away from the Masurian Lakes region farther north. The Battle of Bolimov is mainly remembered today because it saw the first use of poison gas in World War I. The Germans fired shells containing a type of **tear gas**. The experiment failed, as the gas, which was stored as a liquid, could not **vaporize** in the freezing conditions and fell harmlessly to the ground.[14]

SECOND BATTLE OF THE MASURIAN LAKES

Further north, the Second Battle of the Masurian Lakes was fought in the bitterly cold winter of February 1915, between the Russian and German armies. The battle was an attempt by Paul von Hindenburg to bring to an end the fighting on the Eastern Front. The German chief of staff, Erich von Falkenhayn, was reluctant to divert troops from the fighting on the Western Front, but he was won over.[12] The Russians were encircled by the German army and were forced to retreat and flee. Thousands were taken prisoner. Although the battle did not bring a conclusive end to fighting on the Eastern Front, it did finally drive the Russians from East Prussia and end the threat there.[13]

RETREAT AND ATTACK

Throughout the spring and summer of 1915, the Russian army was gradually pushed back by a series of Austro-German **offensives**. By September 1915, the "Great Retreat" was over. Russia had surrendered all of its territories in Poland. However, the retreat had been a skilled one—weapons and other equipment had been dismantled and transported to safe areas, and a large part of the Russian army was still intact.[15]

Most fighting stopped during the winter, but 1916 saw another major offensive on the Eastern Front, this time from the Russians. The Brusilov Offensive, named after General Alexei Brusilov, began on June 4, 1916, along a front that extended 200 miles (320 kilometers) from Lutsk in the north to the border with Romania in the south. The attack took the Austrian army by surprise. Within a month the Russians had made considerable advances and had taken 350,000 Austrian prisoners. More attacks followed into October. Once again, the Central Powers were forced to move troops from the Western Front to fight the Russians. The Brusilov Offensive crippled the Austrian army, but the Russians suffered huge numbers of casualties, too—an estimated 1 million men dead, wounded, or taken prisoner. An exhausted army, along with famine and riots at home, set the scene for the dramatic events of 1917 in Russia: the Russian Revolution.[16]

These Russian prisoners of war are being escorted by German guards.

TSAR NICHOLAS II

Nikolai Aleksandrovich Romanov was born near St. Petersburg, Russia, on May 18, 1868. He was the eldest son of Tsar Alexander III. He succeeded to the throne in 1894, and in the same year he married Princess Alexandra of Hesse-Darmstadt (a territory in Germany). Nicholas was devoted to his wife, and her influence over him was to play a large part in the events that followed.

As tsar, Nicholas was the ruler of a huge empire that stretched from central Europe in the west to the Pacific Ocean in the east. He believed that he derived his authority to rule from God, and these **autocratic** views were strongly reinforced by Alexandra. When, early on in his reign, representatives from various local assemblies asked him for reforms to the government, he dismissed their petitions as "senseless dreams."

CONFLICT WITH JAPAN

Nicholas was eager to expand Russian influence in East Asia, particularly in Manchuria (modern-day northeast China) and Korea. This led Russia into conflict with Japan. In 1904 the Japanese attacked the Russian fleet in Port Arthur, in the Yellow Sea. The war

This family portrait shows Tsar Nicholas II with his wife, Alexandra, and his five children.

that followed was a disaster for Russia, as its troops were forced to retreat through Manchuria, and its Baltic Fleet was destroyed by the Japanese at the Battle of Tsushima. The war caused increasing unrest in Russia. In January 1905, the army opened fire on demonstrators in St. Petersburg. Nicholas was unwilling to make any compromises, but he was eventually forced to accept the creation of a representative assembly, the Duma.

Nicholas and Alexandra had four daughters and one son, Alexei, the heir to the throne. Alexei suffered from hemophilia, a disease that prevented his blood from clotting. At the time, there was no effective medical treatment for the disease. In desperation Alexandra turned increasingly to a mystic monk, Grigori Rasputin, for help. Rasputin gained great power over both Alexandra and Nicholas. He was eventually murdered in 1916.

After the disastrous campaigns of 1915, Nicholas decided against all advice to take on the command of the Russian armies himself. This move meant that every military failure became associated with him personally. Even worse, with Nicholas away from St. Petersburg for much of the time, responsibility for government passed to Alexandra, who was by now firmly under the influence of Rasputin.

Food shortages, poverty, and the massive casualties of war led to increasing unrest. In March 1917, having lost the support of the government and the army, Nicholas was forced to **abdicate**. He and his family were executed in July 1918.

Nicky to Willy

This is one of the letters written by Nicholas (Nicky) to his cousin Kaiser Wilhelm II of Germany to try to avoid the outbreak of war:[17]

Peter's Court, Palace,
August 1, 1914

Sa Majesté l'Empereur Berlin,
I received your telegram. Understand you are obliged to mobilize but wish to have the same guarantee from you as I gave you, that these measures do not mean war and that we shall continue negotiating for the benefit of our countries and universal peace dear to all our hearts. Our long proved friendship must succeed, with God's help, in avoiding bloodshed. Anxiously, full of confidence await your answer.

Nicky

THE WAR AT SEA

The pre-war race to build up the British and German navies was won by the British, who entered the war with a larger and better-equipped navy (see table below). Neither country wanted a direct confrontation between the two fleets, as neither wanted to lose ships in battle. Instead, the Germans planned to use mines and submarine attacks to challenge British supremacy at sea. The main aims of the British navy were to protect vital trade routes into Britain, and to prevent supplies from reaching Germany by enforcing a **blockade** of the North Sea.[1]

Naval strengths in 1914[2]

	Britain	Germany
Dreadnoughts	24	13
Battle cruisers	8	5
Light cruisers	35	33
Submarines	44	38

Here, a ship takes a hit during the Battle of Heligoland.

Room 40

By three extraordinary pieces of luck, the British intelligence services were able to intercept and decode German naval communications throughout the war. In August 1914, a German light cruiser, the *Magdeburg*, ran aground off the Russian coast. A naval code book retrieved from the ship was sent to the Admiralty in London, where code-breakers set to work in an office that became known as "Room 40." In October, another German code book was captured by the Australian navy and sent to Room 40. A short time after, a third code book was pulled up in the fishing nets of a British trawler. It, too, was passed on to the Admiralty. Using all this information, the British intelligence services were frequently able to warn the navy about German plans.[3]

NORTH SEA BATTLES

The first naval engagement of the war took place on August 28, 1914, at Heligoland Bight, off the coast of Germany.[4] In misty conditions, the British navy succeeded in sinking three German light cruisers and a destroyer.[5] In retaliation, in November and again in December, the German fleet bombarded the North Sea ports of Yarmouth, Scarborough, Hartlepool, and Whitby, in England. Despite intelligence from Room 40 (see box above), the British navy did not manage to intercept the German fleet. The British had more success in January 1915, at the Battle of Dogger Bank, fought off the coast of England. Warned once again by Room 40, cruisers of the British fleet sank the German cruiser *Blücher* and badly damaged another ship. This action was enough for Kaiser Wilhelm II to order the German fleet to remain in its home bases.[6]

With their surface fleet confined to port, the Germans concentrated on other means of attack—by **mines** and submarines. They had already had some successes. On September 22, **torpedoes** fired from a German U-boat (*Unterseeboot* is German for "submarine") had sunk three British cruisers. On October 27 a German mine sunk the British battleship *Audacious*.[7] In February 1915, Germany declared unrestricted submarine warfare. This meant German U-boats would attack merchant ships without warning (see page 33). In retaliation, Britain stepped up its blockade of Germany. It banned neutral countries, such as the United States, from trading with Germany.

THE *LUSITANIA*

On May 1, 1915, a passenger liner, the *Lusitania*, left New York with more than 1,200 passengers and 700 crew onboard. Alongside the advertisement for the voyage was a notice from the German Embassy that warned passengers that "vessels flying the flag of Great Britain, or any of her allies, are liable to destruction ... and that travelers sailing in the war zone on ships of Great Britain or her allies do so at their own risk."[8] On May 7, as the ship entered the Irish Channel, a German U-boat torpedoed it. The liner sank and 1,201 people drowned, including 128 U.S. citizens.[9] The sinking caused outrage, particularly in the United States. In August another liner, the *Arabic*, was sunk, again with the loss of U.S. lives. In September 1915, in fear of provoking the United States any further, Germany suspended all of its submarine activity in British waters.[10]

THE BATTLE OF JUTLAND

In January 1916, Admiral Reinhard Scheer took over the command of the German navy. He and many of the captains of the German fleet found it difficult to justify the inactivity of the navy, particularly when the German army was sustaining huge casualties on the battlefields of the Western Front.[11] Scheer decided to take his fleet

WHEN YOU FIRE REMEMBER THIS

ENLIST IN THE NAVY

◁ The outrage over the sinking of the *Lusitania* was used to stir up patriotic feelings in this U.S. propaganda poster.

out into the North Sea once again, in search of action. This decision resulted in the biggest naval battle of World War I, the Battle of Jutland. Once again, the British were helped by intelligence from Room 40, which gave them advance notice of the German plan of battle. This huge battle, fought on May 31, ended indecisively. The British fleet lost several major ships, while the German fleet escaped back to its home ports, but the British remained in control of the North Sea.[12] Again, the German fleet was confined to the safety of its home ports.

SUBMARINE ATTACKS

The second half of 1916 was a time of heated debate in the German high command over whether to reintroduce unrestricted submarine warfare. The stakes were high. Some thought that an all-out attack on merchant shipping would quickly bring Britain to the brink of starvation, while others believed that such attacks would force the United States to enter the war. Eventually, on February 1, 1917, a campaign of unrestricted submarine warfare was declared. The Germans calculated that the blockade could force Britain to the negotiating table before the United States could mobilize. Their gamble nearly paid off. From February to April 1917, U-boats sank more than 500 merchant ships.[13] Only when the Allies introduced a **convoy** system (see box below) did the rate of loss slow down. The United States declared war in April 1917 (see page 48).

Convoys

The solution to U-boat attacks was for merchant ships to sail in armed convoys. Although there was some initial opposition to this plan, it was first tried out in May 1917. Instead of sailing independently, merchant ships were grouped together and surrounded by a protective ring of naval ships. From May onward, regular convoys meant that the number of sinkings declined rapidly. As one U-boat commander remarked: "The oceans at once became bare and empty."[14]

U-BOATS

PRIZE RULES

The sinking of three British cruisers early on in the war (see page 29) demonstrated how dangerous U-boats were against warships. But as weapons to enforce a blockade, U-boats were not at first considered very effective. This was because both the German and British navies operated under "prize rules," an agreement that stated that passenger ships could not be attacked, and that if a merchant ship were attacked, the crew had to be taken off to safety before it was sunk.[15] Attacks under prize rules were completely impractical for U-boats. The submarines were too small to take on prisoners, and it was very risky for them to come to the surface to attack a merchant ship, which might very well try to ram them.

Unrestricted submarine warfare, first declared by the Germans in February 1915, ignored the prize rules. Merchant ships and passenger liners suspected of carrying war supplies were sunk without warning. It was a dangerous tactic, as it risked bringing powerful neutral countries such as the United States into the war. But in 1917, unrestricted submarine warfare very nearly succeeded in crippling Britain.

▽ German U-boats, such as the one below, could inflict terrible damage on enemy warships if the German navy ignored the prize rules.

Q-SHIPS

The British came up with various counter-measures against the U-boat threat, including **decoy** ships, known as Q-ships. These were merchant ships fitted with hidden guns. They carried cargoes of wood and cork that made them almost unsinkable by torpedo. Their aim was to lure the U-boat to the surface, then to drop the panels that concealed the guns and open fire.[16] The first Q-ship to sink a U-boat was HMS *Prince Charles* on July 24, 1915. But the German U-boat commanders soon grew wary of these decoys. British Q-ships were responsible for the sinking of 14 U-boats and damaging another 60. Out of around 200 Q-ships, 27 were lost in action.[17]

Lothar von Arnauld de la Perière, 1886–1941

BORN: Posen (Poznan), Prussia (now part of Poland)

ROLE: U-boat captain from 1915 to 1918

DID YOU KNOW? He was the most successful U-boat captain of World War I. He sank 194 ships, all according to prize rules. He wrote of his wartime experiences: "My record cruise was quite tame and dull. We stopped the vessels. The crews boarded the lifeboats. We inspected the ships' documents, told the crews how they could reach the next port, and then sank the stopped prize."[18]

The commander's story

This account by the commander of a U-boat describes the view through his periscope as a torpedo is launched and hits a merchant ship in 1916:

I saw that the bubble-track of the torpedo had been discovered on the bridge of the steamer.... Then a frightful explosion followed, and we were all thrown against one another by the concussion.... All her [the merchant ship's] decks were visible to me. From all the hatchways a storming, despairing mass of men were fighting their way on deck, grimy stokers, officers, soldiers, groom, cooks. They all rushed, ran, screamed for boats, tore and thrust one another from the ladders leading down to them, fought for the lifebelts, and jostled one another on the sloping deck.[19]

THE WESTERN FRONT

By the end of 1914, the Allies and the Central Powers had fought themselves to a standstill on the Western Front. The Germans had failed to achieve the swift victory in the West dictated by the Schlieffen Plan, and they now adopted a policy of defense. They dug deep and well-constructed trench systems and settled down to defend the territory they had gained during the past few months. The German commander, Erich von Falkenhayn, knew that he needed to concentrate a large number of troops on the Eastern Front, where the Germans were trying to knock the Russians out of the war.

ON THE OFFENSIVE

The French, however, took a very different view of the situation. The land occupied by the Germans contained much of France's natural reserves of coal and iron, and most of its manufacturing industries.[1] For the French it was also a matter of national pride to win back these provinces. The French commander, General Joseph Joffre, was determined to mount attacks on areas of the German front line that seemed vulnerable. He was backed by the British, who were continuing to send large numbers of troops to France, including the first of Minister for War Kitchener's "New Armies" (see page 14). The Allies believed that they could break through the German line at certain vulnerable points. Once the German defenses had been penetrated, the Allies' plan was to attack the railroad lines that kept the German troops supplied with food, equipment, and ammunition.[2]

The French army had launched an offensive in Champagne in December 1914, but this was called off in March after heavy rain had flooded the trenches and made any advance impossible. There were 90,000 French casualties, but no gain in territory. The first major offensive of 1915 was at Neuve Chapelle in March (see the map on page 38). The attack was preceded by a massive **bombardment** of enemy lines that took the Germans completely by surprise. The British troops advanced and made ground quickly as the Germans retreated. But communications between the front line troops and their commanders, about 5 miles (8 kilometers) away, were very slow. By the time new orders arrived, the Germans had taken the opportunity to bring in reinforcements. In this offensive, which lasted three days, there were 11,200 Allied casualties (7,000 British, 4,200 Indian).[3] Once again, there was no significant gain in territory.

Gas attack!

The Germans first used gas as a weapon unsuccessfully on the Eastern Front (see page 24). On April 22, they tried it again at the Second Battle of Ypres. Around 6,000 canisters of chlorine gas were released, sending a dense greenish-yellow cloud toward the Allied trenches. This time the poison gas did its work. Many of the Allied French and Algerian soldiers died in their trenches; some soldiers were taken prisoner, while others fled, blinded and choking. A 4-mile (7-kilometer) gap was left in the Allied front line, but the Germans were so surprised by the success of the attack that they failed to take full advantage of this breakthrough.[4]

▽ These British machine gunners are wearing gas masks to protect themselves from a gas attack.

INDIAN TROOPS ON THE WESTERN FRONT

In 1914 Britain looked to its colonies around the world to provide some of the manpower so desperately needed for fighting the war. India had a large and well-trained army. Two Indian infantry divisions, totaling around 44,000 men, arrived in Marseilles, on the southeast coast of France, in late September and October 1914. Many of these troops were quickly moved north into position to fight in the battles around Ypres (see page 15).

SUFFERING IN THE COLD

The Indian troops had arrived in France dressed in light khaki uniforms, suitable for the hot climate they had come from rather than the cold, wet climate of Belgium and northern France.[5] For them, the cold was a real enemy. As winter set in, many succumbed to frostbite, as well as illnesses such as influenza and pneumonia. They were eventually given thicker, warmer uniforms. The plight of the Indian troops resulted in great sympathy from well-wishers in Britain, who sent gifts of knitted scarves and other items to keep the soldiers warm.[6]

In December 1914, the trenches became so wet and clogged with mud that an order was given for the Indian soldiers to retreat and regroup. Already over 2,000 of their number had been killed.[7] The Indian troops next saw action in March 1915 at Neuve Chapelle (see page 34), where another 4,200 Indian soldiers died in the space of three days. Then, during an offensive near Ypres in April, there were many more casualties as a result of a German gas attack. One Indian soldier wrote in a letter home: "This is not war; it is the ending of the world."[8] The massive casualties suffered by the Indian divisions, combined with the cold, led to a rapid decline in morale. The decision was taken to withdraw the Indian troops from the Western Front, except for two cavalry (mounted) brigades. The Indian cavalry continued to fight bravely on the Western Front until 1918. The infantry, meanwhile, were sent to fight in the warmer climate of Egypt.

INDIAN LABOR CORPS

In addition to the Indian soldiers who fought on the Western Front, around 21,000 Indians also worked in the Labor Corps. This was the organization that provided essential services to the army—for example, cooking, laundry, moving supplies, burying the dead, unloading ships and trains, and repairing roads and railroads.[9] Many of the Labor Corps worked far behind the front lines, but the Indian laborers were often used for more dangerous work close to the action, such as building fortifications or moving ammunition. Today, the names of members of the Indian Labor Corps who died on the Western Front are found alongside those of Indian soldiers in many of the military cemeteries in northern France.

The Royal Pavilion

Many Indian soldiers who were injured in action on the Western Front were taken to Britain for treatment. Some were taken to the Royal Pavilion in Brighton, England, a late 18th-century palace built in an exotic Indian style for the man who would become Britain's King George IV. During World War I, the pavilion was turned into a military hospital specifically for the Indian soldiers, with 742 beds.[10]

Here, soldiers of the Indian army are pictured in France with their bicycles.

This map shows the Western Front from 1914 to 1918. Troops fought across the same areas of land for four years.

VERDUN

At the beginning of 1916, in an attempt to break the French army, the Germans launched a major attack on the French fortress of Verdun, in northeastern France. General von Falkenhayn reasoned that if the Germans could inflict massive casualties, "the forces of France would bleed to death."[11] A knockout blow to the French could, he thought, also bring Britain to its knees.[12] Falkenhayn chose Verdun for the attack because he knew that the fortress was an important status symbol for the French. He counted on the fact that they would defend it fiercely.

Falkenhayn's shrewd calculation was correct. The German assault on Verdun began on February 21. Three days later, the Germans had captured the stronghold of Fort Douaumont, and Verdun looked extremely vulnerable. At that point a new commander, Philippe Pétain, was put in charge of French operations at Verdun. He was determined not to lose the fort. He sent a message to the commander of the troops around Verdun: "I have taken command. Tell your troops. Hold fast."[13] This was exactly what Falkenhayn wanted. Pétain sent in reinforcements along the only supply route to the fort, which came to be known as *la voie sacrée* ("the sacred way"). The fighting dragged on for months, with heavy casualties on both the French and German sides. By the end of June, a total of more than 200,000 men (on both sides) had been killed and injured in the fighting at Verdun.

THE SOMME

In July 1916, attention switched away from Verdun to another part of the Western Front. The Allies had been planning an offensive in the region of the Somme, in northern France, since the beginning of 1916. However, the timing of the attack was brought forward to relieve French forces at Verdun. The British commander in charge of the offensive was Douglas Haig.

BIOGRAPHY

Sir Douglas Haig, 1861–1928

BORN: Edinburgh, Scotland

ROLE: Commander-in-chief of the British Expeditionary Force, 1915–18. He remains a controversial figure because of the huge numbers of casualties sustained under his command at the Battle of the Somme (1916) and at the Third Battle of Ypres (1917, also called Passchendaele). His policy of attrition has been summarized as "kill more Germans."

DID YOU KNOW? After the war, Haig helped to establish the Royal British Legion, an organization dedicated to the care of those who had suffered as a result of service in the armed forces in World War 1. He devoted his life to the welfare of soldiers who had served during the war.[14]

The German trenches along the Somme were deep and well-defended. On June 24, the Allies began a week-long bombing of the German front lines. The shelling was meant to empty the German lines in preparation for a massive Allied attack. Many Germans survived by retreating to their fortifications. On July 1, thousands of Allied troops moved in waves toward the German lines. They expected little or no opposition. In fact, they were met by lethal machine gun fire from the well-protected German positions. Of the 100,000 British soldiers who attacked that day, 20,000 died and another 40,000 were wounded. Despite the appalling loss of life, the Battle of the Somme continued until November 19.[15]

ATTACK AND DEFENSE

In December 1916, General Robert Nivelle became commander of the French forces. Nivelle had taken over from Pétain at Verdun, and he was responsible for the eventual recapture of the fort. He now planned a new Allied offensive for 1917 to squeeze the Germans between two attacks in Champagne and Arras (see the map on page 38). He predicted that the offensive would achieve success within two days.[16] However, as a result of lapses in security, Nivelle's plans became known to the Germans.[17]

In fact, the German commanders, Paul von Hindenburg and Erich von Ludendorff, already had plans of their own. During fall 1916, the Germans had been building a series of linked fortifications up to 30 miles (48 kilometers) behind their own front line. This fortified line was called the Siegfried Line by the Germans, but it became known to the Allies as the Hindenburg Line (after Paul von Hindenburg). During the spring of 1917, the Germans gradually began to move back to the Hindenburg Line. As they retreated, they adopted a "scorched earth" policy—they destroyed everything that might possibly be of use to the Allies. They also laid mines and booby traps to make the area as dangerous as possible for attacking troops. The Hindenburg Line was considerably shorter than the old German front line, and it required fewer soldiers to defend it, freeing up troops to go to the Eastern Front.

THE NIVELLE OFFENSIVE

Despite the German retreat, Nivelle decided to press on with his offensive. On April 9, the Battle of Arras started the offensive well, with Canadian troops capturing Vimy Ridge. But the Germans were forewarned and well-prepared for the French attack along a 50-mile (80-kilometer) front further south in Aisne. In the massacre that followed, the French suffered 187,000 casualties.[18] In the aftermath, morale in the French army was so low that **mutinies** broke out. Among other things, the soldiers demanded better food and more time off. In May 1917, Nivelle was replaced by Pétain, who listened to the soldiers' grievances and gradually restored order in the French army.

War poetry

The grim experience of life in the trenches on the Western Front inspired all sorts of writing, including poetry. Some of the writers were already poets before they went to fight, while others turned to poetry as a much-needed way to express the fear and horrors of their experiences. In his poem "Exposure," Wilfred Owen described freezing winter conditions in a front-line trench at night:

Our brains ache, in the
*   merciless iced east winds*
*   that knife us …*
Wearied we keep awake
*   because the night is*
*   silent …*[19]

△ Like Owen, Seigfried Sassoon (1886–1967) also fought in World War I and expressed his hatred of war through his poetry.

THE CHANGING NATURE OF WARFARE

The trenches of the Western Front were deep ditches. In wet or stony ground where it was difficult to dig deep, a trench often had a sheltering wall, or **parapet**, along the top of the side facing the enemy. The trenches nearest the enemy were known as the "front line," and the area in-between the two front lines was "**no man's land**." This varied in width from several miles in some places to just a few feet in others. Both sides fixed tangles and rolls of barbed wire in no man's land to act as barriers against attack.

The front line trenches were connected by communication trenches to reserve trenches further back. As the war progressed, these trench systems became increasingly complicated. The Germans, in particular, spent a great deal of time and energy building deep trench systems. Some trenches even had wooden bunks and electric light. With more emphasis on offensive tactics, the French and British were less inclined to invest so much effort into building trenches that they hoped not to occupy for long.

KEEP YOUR HEAD DOWN!

The trenches were busiest at night when, under the cover of darkness, troops moved in and out, fetched supplies, and went into no man's land to repair and lay barbed wire or to attempt to collect dead bodies for burial. During the day, movement around the trenches was often dangerous. Even the briefest glimpse over the parapet could result in a bullet through the head from a **sniper's** rifle. Other hazards included flooding and constant mud, lice, trench rats that could grow as big as cats, and "trench fever" caused by the unsanitary conditions.[1]

COMMUNICATIONS

One of the biggest difficulties experienced by both sides during the fighting on the Western Front was communication. All sorts of different methods were employed to relay information and commands, including human runners, signaling lamps, messenger-dogs, and carrier pigeons. Both the Germans and the Allies developed elaborate networks of field telephones. These were connected by wires that were buried beneath trenches or fixed to trench walls. One problem was that the wires were easily broken by **artillery** fire. Another was that as attacking soldiers moved forward, they went even further away from the nearest point of communication. Several offensives failed because commanders had no accurate information about what was actually happening on the ground, and because orders took too long to reach front-line troops.

Radio

The photo below shows German troops operating a field telephone on the Western Front. Radio sets were also used in World War I, but they were large, heavy, and cumbersome. This is an account by a young radio operator describing the moment he is told that he will be going in to attack with the infantry at Arras in 1917:[2]

The attack was to be made within the next few days, the infantry waves were to advance under cover of a formidable barrage, and each wave was to be provided with a wireless [radio] station. The Roclincourt station was to go over with the first infantry wave. The Roclincourt station! That was Hewitt and I and an officer! Four infantrymen were to assist us in carrying our weighty apparatus, the set, accumulators, dry cells, coils of wire, earth mats, ropes, and other details.

WEAPONS

The soldiers on the Western Front were equipped with rifles. A sharp blade, called a **bayonet**, could be attached to the end of the rifle for hand-to-hand combat. Machine guns, which could fire continuous rounds of bullets, were a powerful defensive weapon. Although the early machine guns were cumbersome, requiring a team of four to six men to operate them, their effectiveness was demonstrated in battles such as the Somme, where thousands of attacking Allied troops were mown down by German machine gun fire. Lighter and faster guns were developed as the war progressed.[3] Bombs, **grenades**, **trench mortars**, and flamethrowers were also widely used by the opposing armies.

Behind the front line, the big guns—artillery—were used to bombard the enemy with shells. As the war progressed, a tactic called the "creeping barrage" developed. The idea was for a curtain of shells to fall just ahead of advancing infantry. The aim was to keep the enemies pinned in their trenches. The creeping barrage relied on accurate artillery fire and good communications. This tactic was used with varying degrees of success, notably in the Battle of the Somme and the Second Battle of the Aisne.[4]

NEW IDEAS

The creeping barrage was one of many new ideas that were tried out and developed on the Western Front. Gas attacks, first attempted by the Germans, became widely used by both sides. Soldiers carried gas masks, but different types of poison gas were responsible for thousands of deaths during the war.[5] The most astonishing "new idea" for the troops who watched it first drive into action in 1916 was the tank (see also pages 46–47). The other major innovation of World War I was the use of aircraft.

World War I broke out only a decade after the first successful powered flight. At the beginning of the war, aircraft were considered useful only for **reconnaissance**. Yet the pace of development of aircraft technology during the war was phenomenal. In 1914 France had fewer than 140 military planes. By 1918 it had around 4,500.[6] Planes were widely used on the Western Front for observation, often to guide artillery attacks.[7] But as the war progressed, small fighter aircraft (see box on page 45) battled for control of the sky above the battlegrounds. Bigger planes that could carry bombs were used for ground attacks and for some attacks on cities (see page 57).

△ Here, Baron von Richthofen can be seen in his fighter plane. Richthofen was Germany's top aviator during World War I. He was nicknamed the Red Baron.

Garros and Fokker

Fights in the air began fairly ineffectually, as pilots tried to fire at each other with small guns or rifles. The French pilot Roland Garros was the first to devise a way of protecting the plane's propeller with steel plates so that a machine gun could be fired forward. His invention was successful, but his luck ran out when he was shot down in April 1917, and his plane was captured.[8] However, a Dutchman named Anthony Fokker, who was working for the Germans, came up with a better mechanism—the interrupter gear. This was a timing mechanism that prevented the gun from firing when a propeller blade was in front of it. It was used to great effect by the Germans, while the Allies scrambled to produce a similar mechanism.[9]

THE TANK

The tank was the Allies' secret weapon. Tanks made their first brief appearance at Flers, in France, during the Battle of the Somme in 1916, but their first major role was in the Battle of Cambrai on November 20, 1917 (see the map on page 38). The British and the French independently developed their own tanks during World War I.

This British tank is climbing a slope at Wailly, France, on the Western Front in October 1917.

The tank was developed to break the deadlock of trench warfare. It could move over ground broken by shell holes and force its way through barbed wire. In Britain, the development of this new weapon, known then as a "landship," was championed by Winston Churchill, who established a Landships Committee in 1915. The first prototype, known as "Little Willie," was followed by another, "Big Willie," in 1916. The requirements laid down for the finished tank were a minimum speed of 4 miles (6.5 kilometers) per hour, a range of 20 miles (32 kilometers), and the ability to climb a 5-foot- (1.5-meter-) high parapet and cross an 8-foot (2.5-meter) trench. It should have two machine guns and be unaffected by small-arms fire.[10]

BATTLE OF CAMBRAI

The earliest tanks were extremely unreliable. The 36 tanks used in the attack at Flers terrified the German troops, who had not seen this new weapon before, but virtually all of them broke down.[11] By 1917 the British had 476 tanks available for the attack at Cambrai.[12] This attack was against the Hindenburg Line (see page 40), but the tanks showed their worth as they advanced with the infantry following behind. The author Arthur Conan Doyle described the scene in these words: "The long line of tanks magnified to monstrous size in the dim light of early dawn, the columns of infantry with fixed bayonets who followed them, all advancing in silent order, formed a spectacle which none who took part in it could ever forget."[13] Within hours, the tanks had crossed the fortifications of the Hindenburg Line—the first time the Allies had achieved this feat.[14]

Water carriers

The landship was developed and produced in conditions of utmost secrecy. The body shells of the vehicles looked like tanks that were used to carry water. So when the early models were being shipped to France, they were labeled as "'water carriers for Russia." They were then called "tanks," and this was the name that stuck.[17]

For the crews inside the tanks, conditions were truly appalling. In the cramped, hot interior, the men suffered from engine noise, exhaust fumes, and violent movements as the tank crossed broken ground. Many were violently sick or even lost consciousness. Nevertheless, the success of the tank at Cambrai prompted the Germans to develop their own models, although they produced very few compared to the numbers of tanks built by the Allies. On April 24, 1918, rival tanks met each other for the first time in the war at Villers-Bretonneux. The Allies used tanks for the final assaults on the Hindenburg Line in 1918.[15]

Tank Production, 1916–18[16]

Year	United Kingdom	France	Germany	Italy	United States
1916	150	-	-	-	-
1917	1,277	800	-	-	-
1918	1,391	4,000	20	6	84

THE UNITED STATES ENTERS THE WAR

"If we end up at war with America, we will face an enemy with such moral, financial, and economic strength that we will have nothing more to hope for from the future; that is my firm conviction." These words were written by the German banker Max Warburg in January 1917, at a time when the pros and cons of unrestricted submarine warfare were being hotly debated in Germany (see page 31).[1] Warburg thought the risk of pushing the United States to declare war was too great, but only a small minority in Germany shared his opinion. The return to unrestricted submarine warfare on February 1 caused U.S. President Woodrow Wilson to break off diplomatic relations with Germany two days later. The sinking of several U.S. merchant ships in the following weeks also helped to bring the United States closer to declaring war.

THE ZIMMERMAN TELEGRAM

In February 1917, the British intelligence service passed to President Wilson a telegram that had been sent and intercepted in the previous month. It was from the German foreign minister, Arthur Zimmerman, to the German minister in Mexico. In it, Zimmerman urged Mexico to attack the United States in alliance with Germany if the United States entered the war. The Zimmerman telegram was published on March 1, 1917, to great public outrage in the United States.[2] President Wilson declared war on Germany on April 6, 1917.

NEW OPERATIONS

For the Allies, the entry of the United States into the war was a relief. Germany's policy of unrestricted submarine warfare was alarmingly successful from an Allied point of view. The United States' entry into the war immediately mobilized the powerful U.S. navy, but it was the introduction of the convoy system that curtailed the U-boats' activities. The success of the German U-boats did, however, prompt a new offensive on the Western Front. Britain's General Haig wanted to attack the German lines in Belgium, with the aim of breaking through and destroying the U-boat bases at Ostende and Zeebrugge. This aim led to the Third Battle of Ypres, also known as Passchendaele, which began on July 31, 1917. The fighting dragged on until November, with a small gain for the Allies. Once again the cost in human life was enormous—310,000 Allied and 260,000 German casualties.[3]

The French army played virtually no part in the Third Battle of Ypres. It was still recovering from the casualties of the Nivelle Offensive and the mutinies that followed (see page 41). The overall French strategy had changed from one of offense to defense.[4] As General Pétain said, "We must wait for the Americans and the tanks."

Mud

During the Third Battle of Ypres, heavy summer rain turned the ground to mud. This description of the battlefield was written by a British soldier named Private H. Jeary: "As far as the eye could see was a mass of black mud with shell holes filled with water. Here and there broken duckboards, partly submerged in the quagmire; here and there a horse's carcass sticking out of the water; here and there a corpse."[5]

Shell holes, filled with water and surrounded by a sea of mud, were a common sight at Ypres in 1917.

WOODROW WILSON

As president of the United States when war broke out in Europe in 1914, Woodrow Wilson adopted a stance of neutrality. He saw his role as one of peacemaker and worked actively throughout 1915 and 1916 to try to find a solution to the stalemate. In December 1916, Wilson sent identical peace notes to all the participants in the war, asking each one to state their terms for peace. In January 1917 he gave a speech to the U.S. Senate in which he called for "peace without victory" and outlined his idea for a future league of nations.[6]

A FINE BALANCE

From 1914 to 1917, Wilson skillfully managed to keep his country neutral while continuing to trade with countries involved in the war, notably Great Britain. The Germans' response was to try to disrupt this trade with unrestricted submarine warfare, but they were treading a fine line because they did not want to provoke the United States into declaring war. The sinking of merchant ships and the Zimmerman telegram tipped this balance in 1917. On April 2, Wilson went before Congress to call for a declaration of war. He told Congress that the time for neutrality was over, saying: "The world must be made safe for democracy." In this speech, Wilson made it clear that the United States was going to war for clear moral reasons. By taking the United States into the war, Wilson also hoped to have greater influence over what happened after it ended.

THE 14 POINTS

Wilson continued his diplomatic efforts even after the United States entered the war. In January 1918 he presented Congress with "14 points" on which peace should be negotiated (see page 63 for a summarized list of the 14 points). The last of the points outlined the foundation of a "general association of nations"—the League of Nations—that would give a guarantee of "political independence and territorial integrity to great and small states alike."[7] After the **Armistice** in November 1918 (see page 64), Wilson went in person to Paris to take part in the negotiations for what he hoped would be an enduring peace after the war.

BIOGRAPHY

Thomas Woodrow Wilson, 1856–1924

BORN: Staunton, Virginia

ROLE: Twenty-eighth president of the United States (1913–21). In 1916 Wilson became the first **Democratic** president to win a second term in office since Andrew Jackson in 1832. His slogan as he ran for the presidency was "He kept us out of war," but his victory was also the result of social legislation, such as laws to prohibit child labor and to limit the workday to eight hours for most railroad workers.[8]

DID YOU KNOW? Woodrow Wilson's father was a Presbyterian minister who served as a chaplain for the Confederate Army (southern states) in the Civil War. His church was turned into a military hospital, and the young Woodrow Wilson saw the horrors of war firsthand.[9]

THE AMERICAN EXPEDITIONARY FORCE

In April 1917, the United States had a powerful navy but only a small army of around 108,000.[10] In order to supply the numbers of soldiers needed by the Allies, conscription was introduced in May 1917. The first U.S. troops of the American Expeditionary Force arrived in France in June 1917 with their commander, General John Pershing. Over the following months, thousands more U.S. troops were recruited and trained. By March 1918, there were more than 300,000 U.S. troops, known as "doughboys" on French soil.[11] Pershing was determined that the American Expeditionary Force should fight as a separate unit on the Western Front and not be broken up among the British and French troops. But the Allies became so desperate for manpower in the spring of 1918 that Pershing relented and released some troops to serve under British and French commanders as a temporary measure.

OPERATION MICHAEL

At the end of 1917, fighting on the Eastern Front came to an end, and Russia opened peace negotiations with Germany. The Treaty of Brest-Litovsk between the Central Powers and Russia was signed on March 3, 1918. The commander of the German army, General Erich Ludendorff, began to transfer troops from the Eastern to the Western Front in preparation for one final, all-out attack on the British and the French. He was eager to launch this offensive before the Americans had time to get their troops ready for battle. The main part of Ludendorff's plan, code named "Michael," was to attack the British line on the Somme and push the British forces rapidly toward the English Channel. This would create a gap between the British and the French armies. Ludendorff calculated that if he could crush the British, the French would admit defeat.

Operation Michael began on March 21, 1918. The Germans rapidly broke through the British lines on the Somme and advanced more than 40 miles (65 kilometers). This was the biggest territorial gain on the Western Front since 1914. But the effort of advancing over the broken, devastated ground exhausted the battle-weary German soldiers. Ludendorff called off the attack in early April.

The Lafayette Escadrille

Although U.S. soldiers did not start to arrive officially in France until 1917, many volunteers from the United States were already fighting in the war. Some served in the French Foreign Legion; others worked in the ambulance corps. From 1915 many U.S. pilots enlisted in the French Air Service, and in 1916 they formed their own squadron—the Lafayette Escadrille. Members of the squadron fought over the battlefields of Verdun in 1916 and observed the German retreat to the Hindenburg Line in 1917. The squadron had two lion cubs named "Whiskey" and "Soda" as mascots. In all, 38 U.S. pilots served in the Lafayette Escadrille, which became part of the American Air Service in 1917. The expertise of those pilots who had already flown on the Western Front was invaluable for the new U.S. squadrons. The lion cubs, meanwhile, went to live in a zoo in Paris.[12]

△ Here, members of the Lafayette Escadrille are pictured with their lion cub mascots.

THE HOME FRONT

In Britain, almost the first act of the government after declaring war in 1914 was to pass the Defense of the Realm Act on August 8. This act gave the government wide-ranging powers, including the rights to seize property and resources for the war effort, to imprison without trial, and to censor and control information (see page 16).[1] This law was also used to control many aspects of civilian life—for example, people were not permitted to light bonfires or set off fireworks, to ring church bells, or to buy binoculars.

Get behind
the Girl he left behind him

Join the land army

FOOD SHORTAGES

In December 1916, the British government established a government department that ensured that all suitable land was being cultivated in order to boost food production. The Women's Land Army was set up in response to a shortage of men to work on farms. By 1917 there were over 260,000 women farm laborers.[2]

Fears of food shortages and panic-buying finally led to **rationing** in Britain in 1918. First sugar was rationed, then meat, followed by all basic commodities.

△ This recruiting poster for the Women's Land Army urges people to support women who volunteer to do agricultural work.

In the United States, food shortages were not as much of a concern. Still, in 1917 the U.S. government encouraged its citizens to plant "victory gardens" in their backyards and in parks, playgrounds, and even on rooftops. The additional produce grown in these gardens went to help make up the shortfall in Europe.

LIBERTY BONDS

To raise money for the war effort, the U.S. government decided to issue so-called "Liberty Bonds." These bonds provided a way for the government to borrow money at a low rate of interest. The money would be repaid at a certain fixed time in the future. The bonds raised around $17 billion by the end of the war.[3] The government put a huge amount of effort into promoting the bonds. Millions of posters were printed with slogans such as "Our biggest gun is our liberty bond—do your bit now," or "Beat back the Hun [Germans] with Liberty Bonds." Charlie Chaplin and Mary Pickford were among the many movie stars who made public appearances to promote the bonds. For those who could not afford to buy bonds, the government issued War Savings Stamps for 25 cents and $5.[4]

Anti-German feeling in the United States

For people in the United States, the enemy—Germany—was many thousands of miles away. But millions of Germans had immigrated to the United States during the 19th century. By 1917 there were more than 8 million German-Americans. Some were imprisoned for spying or supporting the German war effort. Most were forced to buy Liberty Bonds to show their loyalty to their adopted country. Many changed their German names to hide their ancestry— for example, changing "Schmidt" to "Smith." Anti-German feeling was reinforced by government propaganda and by tales of Germany's cruel actions in the war.

WOMEN AND THE WAR

The war opened up new opportunities for women in the United States and Britain. Before the war, work considered suitable for women was limited. Large numbers of women were employed in jobs such as cooks or maids.

But as men left their jobs to volunteer for the army, women began to replace them in a wide range of occupations.[5] Initially this caused some problems. There was opposition from those who did not think women capable of doing "men's jobs." The unions that represented the men who had left their jobs to fight also worried about women taking over too many positions. But as the war continued, women took on work in areas ranging from clerical work and education to public transportation, factory assembly lines, and ship-building.[6] Many women from the United States and Britain also supported the war effort by nursing the wounded or working as drivers or telephone operators.

▽ Here, women can be seen at work in an airplane factory in the United States in 1918.

Women and the vote

World War I broke out at a time when many women in the United States and Britain were campaigning for the right to vote. The **suffragettes'** support for the war effort, and the valuable war work being carried out by women generally, did a huge amount to sway public opinion. In 1918 women over 30 years old in Britain were given the right to vote. (It was not until 1928 that women had equal voting rights with men in Britain.) In the United States, women achieved equal voting rights with men in 1920.

ATTACKS ON THE HOME FRONT

The war came to the home front in Britain on January 19, 1915, when a zeppelin bombed Great Yarmouth and King's Lynn on the east coast of England. The raid killed two people and injured 16,[7] and it caused outrage that civilians were being targeted in this way. A zeppelin was a cigar-shaped airship powered by several engines, filled with hydrogen and therefore lighter than air. The Germans used their zeppelins for observation and, increasingly during 1915, for bombing raids.

The first raid on London was in May 1915, and it was followed by many others. The worst was on September 8, 1915, when a zeppelin bombed central London, causing huge amounts of damage. The raid was described by Beatrice Webb in her diaries: "From the balcony we could see shrapnel bursting over the river and behind, somewhat aimlessly. In another few minutes a long sinuous airship appeared high up in the blue black sky, lit up faintly by searchlights…. It moved slowly … the shells bursting far below it—then there were two bursts that seemed nearly to hit it and it disappeared…. It was a gruesome reflection that while we were being pleasantly excited, men, women and children were being killed and maimed."[8]

At first, British defenses were inadequate against the zeppelin threat. But during 1916, improved ammunition—bullets that could rip a hole in the skin of the zeppelin and then set fire to the hydrogen gas inside—were developed. The Germans called off the zeppelin raids in 1917, after 77 out of the fleet of 115 had been destroyed or disabled.[9] Raids over Britain continued, however, now flown by bomber planes.

REPORTING AND PROPAGANDA

About 1917 the U.S. government created posters with the following message: "To Shipbuilders! For the support of our soldiers in France the Government must have at once the ships you are building. Without these ships the war cannot be won. Our Country Looks To You! . . . Help our boys in France. With them win the war."[10] Through these sorts of messages, the government appealed to the emotions and patriotism of Americans, to get support for the war. This was one of several types of propaganda that became popular during World War I.

Picturing the fronts

Allied soldiers were prevented from carrying cameras on the Western Front. Yet some troops still took photographs, a few of which appeared in the newspapers. During the war, many official U.S. and British war photographers were part of the military. Official war artists were also appointed by the British and U.S. governments to depict the war, often while actively serving in the military. Among these artists were Paul Nash, Walter Jack Duncan, Claggett Wilson, and Eric Kennington. Some official photographers were given the job of covering the civilian war effort and the role of women workers.[12]

REPORTING THE WAR

In Britain, the government passed legislation to control all information about military activity. In August 1914, the War Office Press Bureau was set up. It received information from the British army, censored it, and then passed it on to the press. The newspapers wanted to send their own reporters to the front, but this was refused. Instead, Minister for War Kitchener appointed an official journalist from the army. His reports were censored and approved by Kitchener before being released to the press under the byline "Eye Witness."[11]

Concern about these restrictions led the British government to allow selected journalists to become accredited war reporters in 1915. They wore uniforms and were escorted by army officials wherever they went. They were therefore in no position to report accurately or criticize military operations. Like the newspaper owners, they saw their job as very much part of the "war effort."[13]

PROPAGANDA

In Britain, war propaganda was carried out by various government departments until the establishment of the Department of Information in February 1917. Methods of propaganda included the recruiting posters that urged men to join up, as well as pamphlets, movies, and even toys and comics for children.[14] Fear and loathing of the Germans was encouraged with stories of war crimes as the German armies advanced at the beginning of the war.[15]

In the United States, President Wilson was concerned about levels of public support for what was seen as a largely "European" war. Having fought and won an election on the byline "He kept us out of war," Wilson was now faced with the prospect of rallying public opinion to enter the war. In April 1917, he set up the Committee on Public Information (CPI) to promote the war to the American people. Under the leadership of a journalist named George Creel, the CPI used a wide range of propaganda in newspapers, on posters, on the radio, and in movies to get its message across.[16]

▽ Even children's toys had a part to play in wartime propaganda. This child stands proudly in front of a submarine go-cart.

THE END OF THE WAR

Throughout 1916, food and fuel shortages had become an increasing problem in Russia. Growing discontent led to strikes and demonstrations against the tsar and his government. The Russian army, too, was exhausted and demoralized. In February 1917, troops in the Russian capital, Petrograd (St. Petersburg), refused to fire on crowds of demonstrators. This "February Revolution" led to the abdication of Tsar Nicholas II (see page 27) and the establishment of a provisional (temporary) government.[1]

THE OCTOBER REVOLUTION

The minister of war in the new government, Alexander Kerensky, believed a victory on the Eastern Front would gain support for the provisional government. So, in June 1917, he launched a new offensive in Galicia (see the map on page 23) against the Austrian army. The Russians had some initial success against the Austrians, but they were soon brought to a standstill by German reinforcements. Thousands of Russian soldiers, weary of war, deserted their posts. Meanwhile, in Russia, the authority of the provisional government was challenged by the **Bolshevik** Party, led by Vladimir Lenin. In October 1917, the Bolshevik Revolution overthrew the provisional government. This was the beginning of **communist** rule in Russia.

In his "Decree on Peace" (October 26), Lenin proposed a three-month cease-fire and a "just and democratic peace for which the great majority of wearied, tormented, and war-exhausted toilers and laboring classes of all belligerent countries are thirsting."[2] Lenin signed an armistice with the Central Powers on December 15, 1917, followed by the Treaty of Brest-Litovsk on March 3, 1918. Under the terms of the treaty, Russia renounced any claims over Finland and Ukraine, as well as the Baltic states and Poland. The Allies refused to participate in these peace negotiations and the treaty was, in fact, later **annulled** under the terms of the 1918 Armistice (see page 63).[3]

Vladimir Lenin, 1870–1924

BORN: Simbirsk, Russia

ROLE: Founder of the Russian Communist Party and leader of the Bolshevik Revolution in 1917. He studied law, but was arrested for his revolutionary beliefs and sent to Siberia. After this he spent much time in exile in Europe. He became leader of the Bolshevik faction of the Social Democratic Worker's Party. His theories of government, together with those of Karl Marx, formed the backbone of communism. He led the October Revolution in 1917 and, after three years of civil war, the communist government of Soviet Russia.[4]

DID YOU KNOW? Lenin survived an assassination attempt in August 1918 by a member of the Socialist Revolutionary Party. In response, hundreds of political opponents were executed under Lenin's authorization.

THE BEGINNING OF THE END

On the Western Front, the Allies were sufficiently worried by the German gains in Operation Michael (see page 52) to allow the appointment of the French Chief of Staff Ferdinand Foch as supreme commander of the Allied forces. Ludendorff meanwhile persisted with his planned offensive, mounting attacks in Belgium in April and threatening Paris in May. These attacks were initially successful, but the usual problems of keeping the troops supplied, as well as large numbers of casualties, resulted in Ludendorff calling a halt to both.[5]

THE LAST BATTLES

Ludendorff's last attack, the Second Battle of the Marne in July 1918, was his final, desperate attempt to break the Allies. It marked the beginning of the end for the German army. A series of counter-offensives mounted by the Allies started with an attack at Amiens, in northern France, on August 8, led by hundreds of French and British tanks. Ludendorff called this the "black day of the German army."[6] The Germans had reached the end of their resources just as U.S. troops were beginning to arrive in huge numbers on the Western Front. U.S. troops were first involved in an offensive in May at Catigny, in northern France. They fought a successful battle at Le Hamel, in northern France, with Australian troops on July 4. Then, in September, the American Expeditionary Force—this time working as an independent unit—achieved a spectacular victory at St. Mihiel, south of Verdun.[7]

▽ This photograph shows U.S. troops entering the French village of Nonsard in September 1918, following their victory at nearby St. Mihiel.

The 14 Points

In January 1918, President Woodrow Wilson presented Congress with 14 points on which the end of World War 1 should be negotiated.[9] This is a summary of those 14 points:

1. Open covenants of peace [peace treaties], openly arrived at.

2. Freedom of navigation on the seas outside territorial waters in peace and in war.

3. The removal of all economic barriers, and establishment of equality of trade.

4. Guarantees that national armaments will be reduced to the lowest point consistent with domestic safety.

5. A free, open-minded, and absolutely impartial adjustment of all colonial claims, that in determining all such questions ... the interests of the people concerned must have equal weight with the claims of the government whose title is to be determined.

6. The evacuation of all Russian territory.

7. Belgium should be evacuated and restored.

8. All French territory should be freed and the invaded portions restored, and the wrong done to France by Prussia in 1871 in the matter of Alsace-Lorraine ... should be righted...

9. The frontiers of Italy should be readjusted along clearly recognizable lines of nationality.

10. The peoples of Austria-Hungary should have the freest opportunity to independent development.

11. Romania, Serbia, and Montenegro should be evacuated and restored ... and the relations of the several Balkan states to each other should be determined by friendly counsel...

12. The Turkish portion of the Ottoman Empire should have a secure sovereignty [authority], but the other nationalities which are under Turkish rule should have an undoubted security of life and an opportunity of independent development, and the Dardanelles should be permanently opened as passage to the ships and commerce of all nations.

13. An independent Polish state should be erected including the territories inhabited by Polish populations...

14. The League of Nations should be formed.

THE END OF THE GERMAN EMPIRE

By the end of September, Ludendorff and Hindenburg knew that there was no alternative but to seek an armistice. Peace notes were sent to President Wilson asking for the opening of peace negotiations based on the 14 Points. Meanwhile the fighting continued on the Western Front. Although the Allied troops had made significant advances across the Hindenburg Line, they continued to encounter strong resistance. In a complete change of heart, Ludendorff demanded that Germany should continue to fight. But it was too late, and on October 26, Ludendorff resigned.[8]

On November 8, General Foch met the German armistice delegation on a special train in the Forest of Compiègne, near Paris. With revolution threatening on the streets of Germany's cities, the abdication of Kaiser Wilhelm II was announced on November 9 (signed and made official on November 28), and Germany was proclaimed a **republic**.

THE ARMISTICE

The terms of the armistice were harsh. Germany was required to evacuate all occupied land, including Alsace-Lorraine, within two weeks, and to hand over large amounts of war equipment to the Allies. The Treaty of Brest-Livotsk and another treaty with Romania were annulled. Any deviation from the armistice terms would result in the resumption of hostilities within 48 hours. The German negotiators had little choice but to accept—Germany was in no state to continue fighting. The armistice was signed at 5 a.m. on November 11. The war came to an end at 11 a.m. on the same day.[10]

The Allies continued their blockade on Germany into 1919, while the negotiations at the Paris Peace Conference took place. The situation in Germany became desperate. In a telegram sent to Paris, Field Marshal Herbert Plumer, commander of the British Army of Occupation on the Rhine, said: "In my opinion food must be sent into this area by the Allies without delay. The mortality amongst women, children, and the sick is most grave, and sickness due to hunger is spreading. The attitude of the population is becoming one of despair, and the people feel that an end by bullets is preferable to death by starvation."[11] The full blockade only ended when the Treaty of Versailles was eventually signed, on June 28 (see page 66).

REMEMBRANCE THROUGH LITERATURE

Many of those who were caught up in the war wrote about their experiences, whether in diaries, letters or poems, or afterward in **memoirs** and novels.

The years after the war saw the publication of some remarkable works about the war. As a young man, the U.S. author Ernest Hemingway joined a volunteer ambulance unit with the American Red Cross on the Italian front. He was injured in 1918 and was decorated for his bravery by the Italian government. He vividly recalled his experiences in his novel *A Farewell to Arms* (1929), which is told from the perspective of an ambulance driver. The novel explores the incredible human toll of the war.

British author Siegfried Sassoon took a similar view of the war. When his war memoir, *Goodbye to All That*, was published in 1929, it caused controversy because of its grim honesty.

Military casualties

There are no definitive figures for casualties during World War I, but these estimates show the scale of the conflict.[12]

Country	Killed	Wounded or missing
Belgium	44,000	450,000
Great Britain	659,000	2,391,000
France	1,359,000	4,455,000
Russia	1,700,000	5,000,000
United States	58,000	204,000
Austria-Hungary	922,000	3,620,000
Germany	1,600,000	4,168,000
Italy	689,000	959,000
India	43,000	71,000
Canada	57,000	150,000
Australia	58,000	152,000
Turkey	250,000	400,000

WHAT HAVE WE LEARNED?

In early 1919, Allied leaders met in Paris to decide on the terms for peace. It was this meeting that produced the Treaty of Versailles. Four heads of government—David Lloyd George of Britain, Georges Clemenceau of France, Woodrow Wilson of the United States, and Vittorio Orlando of Italy—effectively made all the decisions. The Allies all wanted something slightly different. Wilson envisaged a settlement based on his 14 points, including the establishment of a League of Nations that would provide **collective security**. Britain and France were eager to make the Germans pay for the war, and France was determined to achieve security against future aggression. The Germans themselves were given no say in the treaty that was presented to them in May 1919, which they eventually signed in June.[1]

Total war: A new kind of conflict

It is clear that World War I was a very different kind of war than any experienced before. It was a world war because it involved troops from all parts of the globe, and because the fighting was widespread. It was also the first industrial war. Advances in weapons technology and industrial manufacturing allowed the slaughter of huge numbers of soldiers. The war swallowed up resources—not only the men fighting on the various battle fronts, but also the men and women on the home fronts, working to feed the war effort. The organization of entire societies around the needs of the war became known as "total war."

STABBED IN THE BACK?

The terms of the Treaty of Versailles caused huge resentment in Germany. It imposed a "War Guilt Clause" that allotted blame for the war to Germany and its allies, and as a consequence forced Germany to pay **reparations**. The final amount was not decided until 1921. In addition, Germany lost territory in Europe and overseas, its fleet was surrendered to Britain, conscription was banned, and its army was restricted to 100,000 men. The Allies knew that the Germans would not like the terms, but they calculated that Germany had little choice in defeat.

The problem was that many Germans did not believe that their country had been defeated. No victorious armies had marched into Berlin. Instead, the German soldiers had returned home still looking very much like a fighting force. Encouraged by Ludendorff and others, rumors circulated that the army had been "stabbed in the back"— betrayed and robbed of certain victory by its own government under the influence of socialists and pacifists. These rumors, coupled with the terms of the treaty, provoked fury in Germany.[2]

TOWARD WORLD WAR II

The Allies themselves disagreed about the treaty. In the United States, the Senate, under **Republican** control since the end of 1918, rejected the Treaty of Versailles and negotiated separate peace terms with the Germans. France wanted strict enforcement of the treaty's terms, while Britain adopted a more conciliatory approach. It is clear that this disunity between the Allies was a major factor in failing to contain German power and allowing the rise of nationalism and militarism in Germany in the years that followed. In the 1930s, the rising Nazi leader, Adolf Hitler, violated the terms of the treaty many times, with little opposition from the Allies. The scene was set for the outbreak of another world war.

Even in the 21st century, we are still dealing with problems created by the events of World War I and made worse after World War II— for example, the breakup of the former Yugloslavia, and the impact of decisions made about Arab independence and a Jewish Homeland.

TIMELINE

PRE-WAR

1839 Treaty of Guarantee of Belgian neutrality

1871 Franco-Prussian War ends

1879 Austro-German Treaty

1882 Triple Alliance (Germany, Austria-Hungary, and Italy)

1887 Reinsurance Treaty (Germany and Russia)

1888 Wilhelm II becomes kaiser of German Empire

1890 Bismarck resigns

1894 Franco-Russian Alliance

1902 Anglo-Japanese Alliance

1904 *Entente Cordiale* (France and Britain)

1907 Anglo-Russian Agreement

1908 Bosnian annexation crisis

1912–13 First and Second Balkan Wars

1914

June 28 Archduke Franz Ferdinand assassinated in Sarajevo

July 23 Austria-Hungarian ultimatum to Serbia

July 28 Austro-Hungary declares war on Serbia

Aug. 1 Germany declares war on Russia

Aug. 2 Ultimatum from Germany to Belgium demanding safe passage across Belgian territory

Aug. 3 Germany declares war on France. German army invades Belgium.

Aug. 4 Britain declares war on Germany. President Woodrow Wilson declares U.S. policy of neutrality.

Aug. 6 onward Battle of the Frontiers (Western Front)

Aug. 9–16 British Expeditionary Force lands in France

Aug. 17 Russia invades East Prussia and has initial victory at Stalluponen (Eastern Front)

Aug. 20 Battle of Gumbinnen (Eastern Front)

Aug. 23 Battle of Mons (Western Front). Austria-Hungary invades Russian Poland (Eastern Front).

Aug. 26–30 Battle of Tannenberg (Eastern Front) ends with German victory

Aug. 28 Naval battle of Heligoland Bight

Sept. 6–10 Battle of the Marne ends with German retreat followed by "Race to the Sea" (Western Front)

Sept. 9 First Battle of the Masurian Lakes (Eastern Front)

Oct. 18–Nov. 12 First Battle of Ypres ends with both sides dug into trenches along the Western Front

Oct. 29 Ottoman Empire enters the war on the side of the Central Powers

Dec.–March 1915 French offensive in Champagne (Western Front)

Dec. 25 Unofficial Christmas truce in the trenches (Western Front)

1915

Jan. 19 First zeppelin raid on Britain

Jan. 31 First use of poison gas at Battle of Bolimov (Eastern Front)

Feb. 4 Germany declares unrestricted submarine warfare

Feb. 7–21 Second Battle of the Masurian Lakes (Eastern Front)

Feb. Naval bombardment starts in Dardanelles Strait

March 10 Offensive at Neuve Chapelle (Western Front)

April 22 First use of poison gas on Western Front at Second Battle of Ypres (Western Front)

April 25 Allied landings in Gallipoli

May 7 *Lusitania* is sunk by a German U-boat

Sept. 1 Germany suspends unrestricted submarine warfare

Dec. 7 British government orders evacuation of all troops from Gallipoli

1916

Feb. 21 Start of Battle of Verdun (Western Front)

May 31 Naval Battle of Jutland

June 4 Brusilov Offensive (Eastern Front)

July 1–Nov. 19 Battle of the Somme (Western Front)

1917

Feb. 1 Germany resumes unrestricted submarine warfare

Feb.-April German withdrawal to the Hindenburg Line

Feb. 26 Russian troops refuse to fire on demonstrators in Petrograd

March 1 Publication of the Zimmerman telegram

March 15 Abdication of Tsar Nicholas II

April 3 Lenin arrives in Petrograd

April 6 United States declares war on Germany

April 9 Nivelle Offensive starts with Battle of Arras. Canadian troops capture Vimy Ridge (Western Front).

April–May Failure of Nivelle Offensive results in mutiny in the French army

May 10 First use of convoy system to protect merchant shipping

June First U.S. troops arrive in France

June Kerensky Offensive (Eastern Front)

July 31–Nov. Start of Third Battle of Ypres (Passchendaele) (Western Front)

Oct. 24 October Revolution in Russia

Nov. 20 First mass use of tanks at Battle of Cambrai (Western Front)

Dec. 15 Lenin signs armistice with Central Powers

1918

Jan. 8 President Woodrow Wilson makes "14 points" speech

March 3 Treaty of Brest-Litovsk between the Central Powers and Russia

March 21 Start of German offensive "Operation Michael" (Western Front)

April 3 French Chief of Staff Ferdinand Foch appointed supreme commander of Allied forces

July 4 Australian and U.S. troops defeat Germans at Battle of Hamel (Western Front)

July 15 Start of Second Battle of the Marne (Western Front)

July 16–17 Tsar Nicholas and family assassinated by Bolsheviks

Aug. 8 Allied attack at Amiens (Western Front)

Sept. 12 U.S. forces achieve victory at St. Mihiel (Western Front)

Nov. 8 General Foch meets German armistice delegation in Forest of Compiègne, near Paris

Nov. 9 Kaiser Wilhelm II abdicates (signed Nov. 28)

Nov. 11 Armistice signed and fighting ends at 11 a.m.

1919

Jan. Start of Paris Peace Conference

June 28 Signing of Treaty of Versailles

GLOSSARY

abdicate formally give up a throne (for example, the position of king)

Admiralty department of the British government in charge of the British navy during World War I

alliance union between two groups or countries

Allies Allied Powers, also called the Entente Powers. In World War I, it means the alliance of Britain (and the British Empire), France, and Russia. Other countries who fought with the Allies included Belgium, Serbia, Italy, Japan, Greece, and Romania. The United States never formally joined the alliance, remaining an "Associated Power."

annexation taking over and incorporating territory

annul declare something invalid

Anzac name for Australian and New Zealand troops

armistice agreement to stop fighting for an agreed length of time

artillery large guns that fire shells

attrition process of weakening or exhausting by constant pressure or harassment

autocratic type of rule by someone who has absolute power

Balkans region in southeastern Europe with the Adriatic Sea to the west, the Mediterranean to the south, and the Black Sea to the east

bayonet sharp blade that can be fixed to the end of a rifle

beachhead area of shore in enemy territory secured and defended by landing forces

blockade act of preventing goods and food from entering a particular place

Bolshevik member of the group that split from the Russian Social Democratic Worker's Party in 1903. The Bolsheviks were led by Vladimir Lenin.

bombardment continuous attack with bombs or shells

cavalry soldiers on horseback

censorship act of removing information—for example, from a newspaper or a letter—that is considered to be unacceptable in some way

Central Powers in World War I, the alliance of Germany and Austria-Hungary, later joined by the Ottoman Empire and Bulgaria

chief of staff senior officer in a large organization, such as one of the armed forces

collective security global arrangement designed to prevent or stop wars. Each state in the system agrees that any aggression toward one state is considered to be aggression to all the states, which will then work together to respond to the threat. The League of Nations and the United Nations were founded on the principle of collective security.

colony country or region that is under the control of another country

communist connected to the political theory in which all property is owned by the community and each person contributes and receives according to his or her ability and needs

conscription compulsory service in the armed forces

convoy in World War I, the system used from 1917 onward to protect merchant ships from U-boat attacks by grouping them together and surrounding them with a protective ring of naval ships

counterattack attack made in response to one made by the enemy

decoy something used to imitate something else, in order to mislead

Democrat in the United States, a member of the center-left Democratic Party

division in the armed forces, a large unit usually made up of several regiments or brigades

dreadnought name given to the large, big-gun battleships developed in the run-up to World War I

grenade small bomb that is thrown by hand

imperialism dominance, often by use of military force, of a powerful state over another, usually weaker, state

memoir historical account written from personal experience

mine type of bomb that is placed just below the surface of the ground, or of the sea, that explodes on impact

mobilization act of preparing and organizing troops for active service

munitions military weapons and ammunition

mutiny rebellion against authority, particularly in the armed forces

nationalist person or movement with strong patriotic feelings

neutral not supporting either side in a conflict

no man's land in World War I, the area in between the opposing front-line trenches

offensive military campaign of attack

Ottoman Empire empire that was founded around 1300 by a Turkish prince, Osman, and lasted until 1922. From 1453 its capital was Constantinople (Istanbul).

pacifist person who believes that war and violence cannot be justified

parapet protective wall along the top of a trench

Parliament major law-making body in Britain

pincer being approached or squeezed from two sides

power bloc group of countries that together hold particular influence

propaganda information that is used to promote a political cause or point of view

rationing act of allowing each person to have only a fixed amount of food or other commodities

reconnaissance scouting out an area to gain information

reparations compensation paid for war damage

republic state with a form of government that is controlled by the people

Republican in the United States, a member of the center-right Republican Party

sniper person who shoots very accurately across a long range from a hidden position

socialism political theory that is based on public ownership and cooperative management of resources

suffragette woman who demanded the right to vote through organized protest

tear gas type of gas that causes severe irritation to the eyes

torpedo underwater missile that explodes when it hits its target

treaty formal agreement

trench mortar short gun that fires bombs

tsar name used for the kings of the Russian empire

vaporize turn into vapor (gas)

NOTES ON SOURCES

The War's Origins (pages 4–9)

1. www.britannica.com/ EBchecked/topic/66989/Otto-von-Bismarck/9612/Imperial-chancellor?anchor=ref150183
2. Frank McDonough, *Cambridge Perspectives in History: The Origins of the First and Second World Wars*, Cambridge University Press 1997, 4
3. www.britannica.com/EBchecked/ topic/126237/colonialism
4. Colin Nicolson, *The Longman Companion to the First World War Europe, 1914-1918*, Longman 2001, 8
5. J. Rickard (September 24, 2007), *German Battleship Classes of the First World War*, www.historyofwar.org/ articles/lists_battleship_classes_ German_WWI.html
6. Niall Ferguson, *The Pity of War*, Penguin 1998, 84
7. Nicolson, 26
8. Ibid
9. www.royal-navy.mod.uk/history/ ships/hms-dreadnought-1906/index. htm
10. www.bbc.co.uk/history/british/ britain_wwone/invasion_ww1_01. shtml#four
11. Nicolson, 27
12. Ferguson, 84

1914 (pages 10–17)

1. Ferguson, 146
2. John Keegan, *The First World War*, Hutchinson 1998, 56
3. www.srpska-mreza.com/bookstore/ kosovo/kosovo19.htm
4. McDonough, 15
5. www.firstworldwar.com/source/ austrianultimatum.htm
6. Nicolson, 79
7. Ibid, 63
8. McDonough, 10
9. Nicolson, 95
10. www.1914-1918.net/regular.htm

11. Nicolson, 96
12. David Roberts, *Minds at War: The Poetry and Experience of the First World War*, Saxon Books 1999, 45
13. www.firstworldwar.com/source/ asquithspeechtoparliament.htm
14. Ferguson, 177
15. www.spartacus.schoolnet.co.uk/ FWWudc.htm
16. www.nationalarchives.gov.uk/ pathways/firstworldwar/first_world_ war/britain_outbreak_war.htm
17. Peter Vansittart, *Voices from the Great War*, Penguin 1983, 28
18. Roberts, 54
19. www.archive.org/stream/warthatwill endwa00welluoft/warthatwillend wa00welluoft_djvu.txt
20. www.firstworldwar.com/posters/ uk.htm
21. www.1914-1918.net/kitcheners.htm
22. Ferguson, 198

The Dardanelles and Gallipoli (pages 18–21)

1. www.firstworldwar.com/timeline/ 1914.htm
2. www.nationalarchives.gov.uk/path ways/firstworldwar/battles/gallipoli. htm
3. Nicolson, 120
4. Nicolson, 123
5. Keegan, 269
6. www.awm.gov.au/commemoration/ anzac/anzac_tradition.asp
7. www.bbc.co.uk/history/worldwars/ wwone/australia_01.shtml
8. www.anzacsite.gov.au/5environment/ vc/biography.html
9. www.anzacsite.gov.au/5environment/ vc/jakka.html
10. www.anzacsite.gov.au/5environment/ vc/biography.html

The Eastern Front (pages 22–27)

1. Norman Stone, *The Eastern Front 1914-1917*, Penguin 1998, 33
2. Stone, 35
3. Ibid, 40, 43
4. Ferguson, 96
5. Stone, 17
6. Ibid, 23, 49
7. www.britannica.com/EBchecked/topic/648646/World-War-I
8. Nicolson, 106
9. Keegan, 107
10. www.firstworldwar.com/battles/masurian1.htm
11. Nicolson, 108
12. Keegan, 185
13. Ibid, 186
14. www.historyofwar.org/articles/battles_bolimov.html
15. Nicolson, 110
16. Ibid, 111
17. www.firstworldwar.com/source/willynicky.htm

The War at Sea (pages 28–33)

1. www.britannica.com/EBchecked/topic/648646/World-War-I
2. Nicholson, 64
3. www.britannica.com/EBchecked/topic/648646/World-War-I
4. Keegan, 285–6
5. www.firstworldwar.com/battles/heliogoland.htm
6. Keegan, 285
7. Keegan, 286
8. www.firstworldwar.com/features/lusitania.htm
9. Keegan, 287
10. Nicolson, 125
11. Keegan, 290
12. www.britannica.com/EBchecked/topic/648646/World-War-I
13. Ibid
14. www.iwm.org.uk/searchlight/server.php?show=nav.24361&do=media
15. www.iwm.org.uk/searchlight/server.php?show=nav.24361
16. www.uboat.net/history/wwi/part3.htm
17. Ibid
18. www.uboat.net/wwi/men/commanders/10.html
19. Adolf K.G.E. von Spiegel, U-boat 202 (1919)

The Western Front (pages 34–41)

1. Keegan, 197
2. Ibid, 207
3. Ibid, 211
4. Ibid, 214
5. www.black-history.org.uk/pavilionindian.asp
6. Lyn MacDonald, *1915: The Death of Innocence*, Penguin 1993, 66
7. www.westernfrontassociation.com/great-war-on-land/43-britain-allies/252-indian-army-western-front.html
8. www.bbc.co.uk/history/worldwars/wwone/india_wwone_01.shtml
9. www.westernfrontassociation.com/great-war-on-land/113-general-interest/810-labour-corps-pioneers.html
10. www.brighton-hove-rpml.org.uk/HistoryAndCollections/collectionsthemes/pavilionindianhospitalartphotography/Pages/home.aspx
11. Alistair Horne, *The Price of Glory Verdun 1916*, Penguin 1993, 36
12. Keegan, 300
13. Ibid, 304
14. www.britannica.com/EBchecked/topic/251766/Douglas-Haig-1st-Earl-Haig
15. Keegan, 317
16. Ibid, 349
17. www.westernfrontassociation.com/great-war-on-land/65-germany-allies/235-germ-hind-line.html
18. www.firstworldwar.com/battles/aisne2.htm
19. Wilfred Owen, "Exposure," in George Walter (ed.), *The Penguin Book of First World War Poetry*, Penguin 2006, 55.

The Changing Nature of Warfare (pages 42–47)

1. www.firstworldwar.com/atoz/rats.htm
2. www.firstworldwar.com/diaries/awirelessoperator.htm
3. www.firstworldwar.com/weaponry/machineguns.htm
4. www.firstworldwar.com/atoz/creepingbarrage.htm
5. www.firstworldwar.com/weaponry/gas.htm

6. www.theaerodrome.com/aircraft/statistics.php
7. www.firstworldwar.com/airwar/observation.htm
8. www.firstworldwar.com/airwar/deflectorgear.htm
9. www.firstworldwar.com/bio/fokker.htm
10. www.firstworldwar.com/weaponry/tanks.htm
11. Keegan, 320
12. www.1914-1918.net/bat21.htm
13. www.firstworldwar.com/source/cambrai_conandoyle.htm
14. www.firstworldwar.com/battles/cambrai.htm
15. www.1914-1918.net/tanks.htm
16. www.firstworldwar.com/weaponry/tanks.htm
17. www.national-army-museum.ac.uk/exhibitions/permanent-galleries/world-wars-1905-1945/did-you-know

The United States Enters the War (pages 48–53)
1. Ferguson, 284
2. Nicolson, 197
3. www.firstworldwar.com/battles/ypres3.htm
4. Nicolson, 102
5. Lyn MacDonald, *1914–1918: Voices and Images of the Great War*, Penguin 1991, 255
6. Nicolson, 224
7. www.firstworldwar.com/source/fourteenpoints.htm
8. http://millercenter.org/president/keyevents/wilson
9. www.woodrowwilson.org/index.php/woodrow-wilson-biography
10. Keegan, 379
11. Keegan, 401
12. www.neam.org/lafescweb/index.html

The Home Front (pages 54–59)
1. www.bbc.co.uk/history/trail/wars_conflict/home_front/the_home_front_05.shtml
2. www.spartacus.schoolnet.co.uk/Wland.htm
3. www.sossi.org/journal/scouts-ww1-liberty-bonds.pdf
4. www.firstworldwar.com/posters/United States.htm

5. www.bbc.co.uk/history/british/britain_wwone/women_employment_01.shtml
6. www.makingthemodernworld.org.uk/stories/the_age_of_the_mass/04.ST.01/?scene=6
7. www.firstworldwar.com/airwar/bombers_zeppelins.htm
8. www.bbc.co.uk/history/trail/wars_conflict/home_front/the_home_front_06.shtml
9. www.nationalarchives.gov.uk/education/lesson32.htm
10. www.ww1propaganda.com/ww1-poster/shipbuilders-our-country-looks-you
11. Ferguson, 223
12. www.iwm.org.uk/upload/package/95/collections/photographs/1914-1919.html
13. www.bbc.co.uk/history/british/britain_wwone/war_media_01.shtml
14. Ferguson, 228
15. Ibid, 232
16. www.firstworldwar.com/features/propaganda.htm

The End of the War (pages 60–65)
1. www.britannica.com/EBchecked/topic/648646/World-War-I
2. www.bbc.co.uk/history/worldwars/wwone/eastern_front_01.shtml
3. Nicolson, 223
4. www.bbc.co.uk/history/historic_figures/lenin_vladimir.shtml
   www.britannica.com/EBchecked/topic/335881/Vladimir-Ilich-Lenin
5. Nicolson, 104
6. Keegan, 442
7. www.spartacus.schoolnet.co.uk/FWWmihiel.htm
8. Keegan, 446
9. Nicolson, 224
10. Keegan, 447
11. www.ashatteredpeace.com/chapter9.html
12. www.firstworldwar.com/features/casualties.htm

What Have We Learned? (pages 66–67)
1. www.bbc.co.uk/history/worldwars/wwone/versailles_01.shtml
2. Ibid

BIBLIOGRAPHY

BOOKS

Arthur, Max. *Last Post*. London: Penguin, 2006.

Cave, Nigel. *Vimy Ridge: Arras*. Barnsley, England: Leo Cooper, 1997.

Ferguson, Niall. *The Pity of War*. London: Penguin, 1998.

Giddings, Robert. *The War Poets*. London: Bloomsbury, 1988.

Holt, Tonie, and Valmai Holt. *Major and Mrs. Holt's Battlefield Guide to Ypres Salient*. Barnsley, England: Leo Cooper, 2000.

Horne, Alistair. *The Price of Glory: Verdun 1916*. London: Penguin, 1993.

Keegan, John. *The First World War*. London: Hutchinson, 1998.

Macdonald, Lyn. *1914–1918: Voices and Images of the Great War*. London: Penguin, 1991.

MacDonald, Lyn. *1915: The Death of Innocence*. London: Penguin, 1993.

MacDonald, Lyn. *The Roses of No Man's Land*. London: Penguin, 1993.

MacDonald, Lyn. *They Called It Passchendaele*. London: Penguin, 1993.

McDonough, Frank. *Cambridge Perspectives in History: The Origins of the First and Second World Wars*. Cambridge, England: Cambridge University Press, 1997.

Middlebrook, Martin. *The First Day on the Somme 1 July 1916*. London: Penguin, 1984.

Middlebrook, Martin, and Mary Middlebrook. *The Somme Battlefields*. London: Penguin, 1994.

Nicolson, Colin. *The Longman Companion to the First World War Europe, 1914–1918*. London: Longman, 2001.

Noakes, Vivien. *Voices of Silence*. Stroud, England: Sutton Publishing, 2006.

Reed, Paul. *Walking the Salient*. Barnsley, England: Leo Cooper, 1999.

Roberts, David. *Minds at War: The Poetry and Experience of the First World War*. Chicago: Saxon Books, 1999.

Stone, Norman. *The Eastern Front, 1914–1917*. London: Penguin, 1998.

Vansittart, Peter. *Voices from the Great War*. London: Penguin, 1983.

FIND OUT MORE

BOOKS

General World War I history

Barber, Nicola. *Questioning History: The Western Front.* North Mankato, Minn.: Smart Apple Media, 2004.

Brocklehurst, Ruth, and Henry Brook. *The Usborne Introduction to the First World War.* New York: Scholastic, 2007.

Connolly, Sean. *Witness to History: World War I.* Chicago: Heinemann Library, 2003.

Doeden, Matt. *Weapons of War: Weapons of World War I.* North Mankato, Minn.: Capstone, 2009.

Freedman, Russell. *The War to End All Wars: World War I.* Boston: Clarion, 2010.

Heinrichs, Ann. *Voices of World War I: Stories from the Trenches.* North Mankato, Minn.: Capstone, 2011.

Howard, Michael. *The First World War: A Very Short Introduction.* New York: Oxford University Press, 2007.

Worth, Richard. *Wars That Changed American History: America in World War I.* Milwaukee: World Almanac Library, 2007.

The role of women in World War I

Atkinson, Diane. *Elsie and Mairi Go to War: Two Extraordinary Women on the Western Front.* New York: Pegasus, 2010.

Zeinert, Karen. *Those Extraordinary Women of World War I.* Brookfield, Conn.: Millbrook, 2001.

Memoirs, fiction, and primary sources about World War I

Hemingway, Ernest. *A Farewell to Arms.* New York: Simon and Schuster, 2006 (first published 1929).

Morpurgo, Michael. *War Horse.* New York: Scholastic, 2010.

Pendergast, Tom, Sara Pendergast, and Christine Slovey. *World War I Primary Sources.* Detroit: UXL, 2002.

Scherer, Glenn, and Marty Fletcher. *Primary Source Accounts of World War I.* Berkeley Heights, N.J.: Enslow, 2006.

WEBSITES

www.pbs.org/greatwar/
This PBS website contains a timeline, maps, and more and offers a variety of perspectives on the causes and consequences of World War I.

www.firstworldwar.com
Learn more about all the major battles, major figures, and more at this website.

http://wwi.lib.byu.edu/
This website contains links to a variety of fascinating primary sources from World War I, such as diaries and photographs.

www.uboat.net/index.html
This website is about German U-boats in both world wars.

www.westernfrontassociation.com
This is the website of the Western Front Association.

www.1914-1918.net
This website is about the British Army in World War I. It gives detailed information about the army and soldiers' experiences.

www.neam.org/lafescweb/index.html
This website contains information about the Lafayette Escadrille.

INDEX